THE GOSPEL WAY CATECHISM

TREVIN WAX
AND THOMAS WEST

HARVEST HOUSE PUBLISHERS
EUGENE, OREGON

Cover design and illustration by Faceout Studio, Spencer Fuller
Interior illustrations by Spencer Fuller
Interior design by Janelle Coury

For bulk, special sales, or ministry purchases, please call 1-800-547-8979.
Email: CustomerService@hhpbooks.com

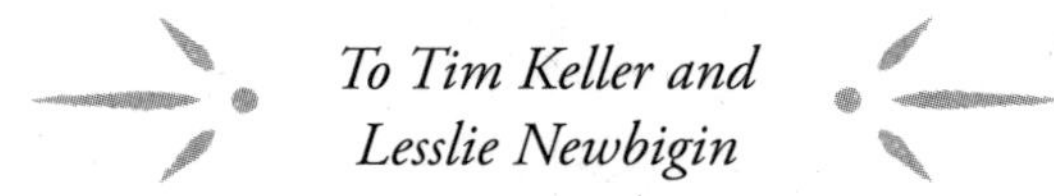

To Tim Keller and
Lesslie Newbigin

The Gospel Way Catechism

Published by Harvest House Publishers
Eugene, Oregon 97408
www.HarvestHousePublishers.com

ISBN 978-0-7369-9141-4 (pbk)
ISBN 978-0-7369-9142-1 (eBook)

Library of Congress Control Number: 2024946103

Printed in the United States of America

25 26 27 28 29 30 31 32 33 / VP / 10 9 8 7 6 5 4 3 2 1

CONTENTS

Introduction

Why Counter-Catechism?

LESSLIE NEWBIGIN WAS A BRITISH missionary and theologian. Born in Newcastle upon Tyne and educated for two degrees at Cambridge, he was commissioned to India as a Church of Scotland missionary and lived abroad for 40 years. Newbigin was an evangelist, community activist, church planter, and organizational strategist.

In 1974, Lesslie and his wife, Helen, retired from full-time missionary work. To celebrate this milestone, they took the long way home. Instead of flying in an airplane, they took a slower 40-day journey of rickshaws, cars, trains, and boats to travel home through Europe. Upon returning to England, the Newbigins were shocked to visit many old towns—once strongholds of Christian thought, now reduced to spiritual rubble. Lesslie recognized how a strong Christian heritage could nearly disappear.[1]

Arriving in London, the Newbigins were surprised to see widespread spiritual apathy. The church's lack of missionary urgency was matched by a way of life that was overly adapted and accommodating to the surrounding society. As he considered the challenges facing the church in his time, Newbigin asked a question that still resonates today: "What if instead of trying to explain the gospel in terms of our culture, we tried to explain our culture in light of the gospel?"[2]

A Church Under the Influence

Today, the church is too often under the influence, drugged by worldly philosophies and practices, sluggish in our witness and evangelism, diminished in our impact as salt and light. Cultural narratives in the West are so powerful they make it hard for the people of God to see straight. We struggle to see things as they are, to understand the difference between truth and error, and to live true to our identity. The secular script of "expressive individualism"—an outlook that describes our purpose in life as looking within to find ourselves and then express ourselves to the world—is prevalent now, to the point we're unaware of just how pervasive this way of looking at the world has become.[3]

This new cultural landscape requires new tactics to contend for the gospel. Newbigin said, "It is not enough for the church to repeat the same words and phrases in different cultural situations. New ways have to be found of stating the essential Trinitarian faith."[4] Like Newbigin, and like countless other Christians seeking to be faithful to the Lord Jesus in their own time and place, we want to rearticulate what we believe in fresh terms. We want to expound the Christian faith in response to new challenges, fresh questions, and the perceived contradictions in this cultural moment.

A Catechism for a Secular Age

One way of meeting the challenges of our day is to take an ancient practice and employ it afresh, to help the church recover what we believe in both depth and breadth. *Catechesis* simply means "instruction." A catechism is one way instruction takes place. Almost every denomination and tradition in church history has used some form of catechesis for the religious education of Christian children and adults: Lutherans (with *Luther's Small Catechism*), Presbyterians (with *The Westminster Shorter Catechism*), Baptists (with *Keach's Catechism*), Catholics (with *Catechism of the Catholic Church*), and Anglicans (with books like J.I. Packer's *To Be a Christian* and *The Catechism of the Book of Common Prayer*).

In the Reformation era, catechisms presented Protestant beliefs over against the teachings of the Roman Catholic Church of the time. These were exercises in counter-catechesis, in that they not only provided a positive vision of Christianity but also sought to oppose the dominant religious options at the time.

Counter-catechesis is a way of presenting Christian truth *as opposed* to the dominant beliefs of a society. What outlook defines our culture today? A secularism that marginalizes and privatizes religious faith and authority; a built-in bias against transcendence and the supernatural; a radical commitment to individualism, pluralism, and skepticism; an openness to all kinds of personal spiritualities that start with the self and not with God. Counter-catechesis is a way of saying, Christianity is not *this,* but *that.* It's saying, *Here's what the world says, but look at what the Bible says.* It's also saying, *You think what you've heard is good, but let me show you how Christianity is better.* Tim Keller was right when he said, "We need a counter-catechism that explains, refutes, and re-narrates the world's catechisms to Christians."[5] The Christian story told in the Bible needs to be taught alongside and even against the secular narratives of the day.

The Gospel Way

In *The Gospel Way Catechism*, we offer the old truths of Christianity in a way that identifies cultural narratives so they can be seen and considered, affirmed for the ways that they rightly embody some aspect of the biblical story, subverted and critiqued for not going far enough in delivering our deep desires of joy and fulfillment, and finally shown only to be fulfilled in and through Jesus Christ. We call this *The Gospel Way* because we trust in Jesus, who claimed to be the Way, the Truth, and the Life (John 14:6). In a world of competing narratives and shifting values, we follow in the footsteps of the early Christians, who described their community as The Way (Acts 9:2)—men and women who walked the path of discipleship in obedience to their King.

Catechisms are tools for thought, study, and memorization. We believe the problem in the church is not that we've asked too much of people but too little. We are inspired by Keller's vision of finding new ways of providing instruction for Christians. He said:

> Christian education, in general, needs to be massively redone. We must not merely explain Christian doctrine to children, youth, and adults but use Christian doctrine to subvert the baseline cultural narratives to which believers are exposed in powerful ways daily. We should distribute this material widely to all, disrupting existing channels, flooding society, as it were, with the material as well as directly incorporating it into local churches.[6]

The word *disciple* simply means student, and we envision the church as a formative and holistic learning community, not merely an inspirational gathering or performance attended only a couple times a month. For the longtime Christian, a counter-catechism can provide a tune-up of sorts, a reminder of how distinct and wonderful the Christian faith is. For the new believer, a counter-catechism can introduce the basics of the Christian faith in distinction to what we experience as common-sense beliefs and practices in the world.

Christianity is not simply something we look *at* but a lens we look *through* to understand our world. We need to recover the scriptural story as *the* story we look through to make sense of the world in which we live. We pray this resource will be an aid to that end.

How to Use This Resource

This is a short book, but it's not something to breeze through. It's packed with concentrated truth. Working your way through a catechism is a process designed for slowness and contemplation, not speed and superficiality. Here are a few suggestions on how to make the most of this resource.

- **Memorize:** Catechism questions and answers are designed to be memorized. There is a rhythm and art to the wording, intended to aid the memory. We recommend spending 5-10 minutes every day for a full week with each question, carefully considering the answer, committing it to memory so you can recite it word for word.
- **Go deeper:** The commentary for each question explains the concepts in fuller detail, showing how Christianity stands in contrast to what often passes for common sense in the world today. We recommend reading the commentary at the beginning of the week, and then again at the end of the week (once you've memorized the answer).
- **Reflect:** Reflection questions give you an opportunity to look at your life in light of Christian teaching and then look for ways to apply the truth to your life. We recommend you work through the reflection questions at the end of the week before moving on to the next question and answer. Pray through this part of the process.
- **Scripture:** Throughout the week, as you have time, look up some of the scripture references, perhaps one or two each day, so you can see how God's Word is the basis for the Christian truths expounded here.

- **Find a partner or group:** One of the best ways to work through a catechism is with brothers and sisters in your church. We recommend enlisting a partner to walk through the process at the same time, for accountability and inspiration, or joining a church group that commits to this process for 50 weeks. Discussing the Christian faith with others will solidify these truths in ways that going solo will not.

PART 1

God

This catechism begins with a section about God, not about us. Why? Because God is the center and point of everything. The world's catechism begins with us; we begin with God. The world teaches that our *self* is found by looking inward to discover our identity and destiny. The Bible teaches that we look upward to God and allow him to narrate our story for us.

God is the ultimate reality around which all creation revolves. He is not a distant deity but intimately involved with his creation, revealing himself so we can see and know him. Through Scripture, nature, and, supremely, through Jesus Christ, we understand who God is and how he desires to relate to us.

God exists as one being in three persons: the Father, the Son, and the Holy Spirit. This triune nature means God is relational, loving, and eternally self-sufficient. The Trinity is a core concept for this catechism, and we'll engage with it extensively in the sections that follow.

God the Father is the Creator, Sustainer, and Sovereign over all. He is holy, just, and loving, guiding history according to his perfect will and purpose. The Son of God, Jesus Christ, is the eternal Word made flesh. He reveals God through his life, teachings, death, and resurrection. Jesus is the Savior who redeems us from sin and the mediator who reconciles us to the Father. God the Holy Spirit is the presence of God active in the world today, indwelling believers, empowering them for godly living, and guiding them into all truth. The Spirit comforts, convicts, and transforms us into the image of Jesus Christ. The world begins with *self*. We begin with God.

QUESTION 1
What Is the Center and Point of Everything?

ANSWER

God is the center and point of everything. In him, all things come to be and are held together. He has no rival.

"I AM THE MASTER OF my fate and the captain of my soul." These words, spoken by Morgan Freeman as Nelson Mandela in the movie *Invictus*, come from the English poet William Ernest Henley.[1] This phrase resonates with us in the modern world, stirring up a sense of exhilaration at the idea of controlling our destiny or determining our own meaning of life. This is one of the controlling ideas in Western culture today. The philosopher Charles Taylor describes this outlook: "My ultimate purposes are those which arise within me; the crucial meanings of things are those defined in my responses to them."[2] *Master of my fate! Captain of my soul! The meaning of life is whatever I make of it. My future is in my hands.*

Exhilaration eventually slides into exhaustion. When we prioritize our individual interests and perspectives above all else, when the "I" is always in the driver's seat, we create a culture lacking in empathy and consideration for others. Loneliness arises. Friendships become shallow. We suffer under the weight and pressure of constantly having to figure out who we are, what our future should be, and what will make us happy.

When looking at life, the world starts with *us.* The Bible starts with *God.* The contrast matters. The Bible pushes back against an overly individualistic, human-centered way of thinking and living. Instead of making meaning, defining our identity, and coming to God on our own terms, we discover meaning, receive an identity, and meet the God who comes to us on *his* terms.

The Bible begins with God because God is the beginning and end. The world doesn't revolve around us, and neither does God. It is *we* who revolve around *him*. And even if we may bristle at being demoted from first place, there's something refreshing to realize God is at the center so that everything else falls into place. The good news of God being the point of everything is that we now have someone outside ourselves who tells us who we are, who declares our worth, and who helps us see the point of our existence.

Instead of living in an inconsistent, risky, and exhausting manner of thinking life is all about us, laboring to make sense of everything independently, why not embrace God as the center and point of everything? Why not experience the sigh of relief as we move out of the center and see God take his rightful place?

The world's catechism says, "You come first." But the Bible says, *Seek God first* (Matthew 6:33). And God promises, "You will seek me and find me when you search for me with all your heart" (Jeremiah 29:13). God can't be reduced to just one of the many priorities on your list; he must be *the* priority. God is not just a chapter in the story of your life; he's the author of your story, the one who makes sense of all the chapters of your life.

God is the master of our fate. God is to be the captain of our souls. "In the beginning, *God*" (Genesis 1:1). The Bible starts with God. So do we.

REFLECTION QUESTIONS

1. **How does acknowledging God as the center and point of everything challenge the contemporary notion that life is all about us?** The idea that we find meaning and purpose inside ourselves stands in contrast to the biblical teaching that meaning and purpose come from God. How does this truth shape your understanding of your identity and purpose?

2. **What risks and pressures are associated with trying to be the "master of your fate" and the "captain of your soul"?** Consider how self-assertion and identity creation can lead to confusion or exhaustion. How does the biblical view of acknowledging God at the center offer a more stable and fulfilling alternative?

3. **What practices can help remind us that God is worthy to be first in our lives?** What are some practical ways our lives can show others that he is the center and point of everything?

SCRIPTURE REFERENCES

- Genesis 1:1
- Psalm 46:10
  Psalm 90:2
- Isaiah 43:10-11
  Isaiah 45:5-6
- Jeremiah 29:13
- Matthew 6:33
- John 1:3
- Romans 11:36
- Colossians 1:16-17
- Hebrews 1:3
- Revelation 4:11

QUESTION 2

How Do We See God and Come to Know Him?

ANSWER

We see God by the light of his revelation, not by our imagination. God reveals his character and purposes through his Word and works.

THE ANCIENT PHILOSOPHER PROTAGORAS SAID, "Man is the measure of all things."[1] This old proverb seems like common sense to many people today. We set the standard. We determine morality. We reject the idea of a cosmic order to which we must conform, as if there could be one story of reality that must be true for all. Instead of looking to God to define the world for us, the individual constructs reality. This is an important aspect of the modern secular vision of life: we don't find meaning *out there;* we create meaning *in here.* If people choose to believe in God, that's fine because God is whoever we imagine God to be.

The Bible points us in a different direction—toward God's revelation of himself. And the Bible presents us with a choice: we can either seek to interpret the world through the story told in the Scriptures or through the story of self. These two visions are rivals, offering fundamentally different ways of understanding reality and human nature. They give different answers to questions about the origins of the world, the nature of humanity, the ultimate purpose of life, the source of moral values, and what happens after death.

As we will see, the story told in the Scriptures begins with creation. The Bible tells us about God's relationship with humanity, our fall into sin, redemption through Jesus Christ, and the ultimate restoration of all things. In contrast, the story of the self relies on natural causes to explain our origins. It emphasizes human autonomy and the notion that we can solve most or all of our problems through science and technology. The story of the self begins and ends with human reason. The story of the Scriptures begins and ends with divine revelation.

In the previous question, we saw that God is the center and point of everything. Now, we ask: How do we see this God? How do we know him? The answer is twofold: through general revelation and through special revelation. General revelation refers to the work of God in creation. Look around at the world and you see something of God's character and attributes. Creation bears his fingerprints. General revelation is wonderful, but it only takes us so far.

Special revelation refers to God's Word (the Bible). We see God most clearly in how he reveals himself through his Word. It's ultimately in Scripture where we come to understand who God is and what he has revealed about himself.

Over the centuries, pastors and theologians have leaned on the metaphor of spectacles or lenses to explain how the Bible functions.[2] The Bible provides a framework or perspective through which we can understand reality, just as glasses or lenses help us see clearly. Only through the lens of Scripture can we truly understand and interpret the world and our experiences. We don't merely look *at* the Bible but *through* it to understand our lives and the world we inhabit. The story of the Scriptures is the lens we use to see God and the world.

In the end, we know God because God has made himself known. We do not conjure up God as we'd like to imagine; we encounter God as he has revealed himself.

REFLECTION QUESTIONS

1. **How does seeing life through the story told in the Scriptures differ from seeing life through the story of self?** Reflect on Protagoras's statement, "Man is the measure of all things," and how this contrasts with the biblical perspective of God's revelation as the ultimate truth. How does each perspective shape one's understanding of reality and morality?

2. **In what ways has the Bible provided you with a clearer understanding of God's character and his purpose for your life?** Consider specific instances in which Scripture has illuminated aspects of God's nature or guided your decisions and actions. How has God's Word helped you see beyond your perceptions and experiences?

3. **How can you apply the metaphor of the Bible as spectacles to your daily life and decision-making?** Consider how regular engagement with Scripture can influence how you interpret events, make choices, and interact with others. How does the study of God's Word help you align your life closely with God's will and purpose?

SCRIPTURE REFERENCES

- Psalm 19:1-2
  Psalm 119:18, 105
- Isaiah 40:8
- John 1:18
- Romans 1:20
- Colossians 1:15-16
- 2 Timothy 3:16-17
- Hebrews 1:1-2
- 2 Peter 1:20-21

QUESTION 3

Who Does God Reveal Himself to Be?

ANSWER

He is the Lord, the great I AM, one God in three persons: Father, Son, and Spirit. He is the Creator and Ruler of all that is, seen and unseen.

MORE THAN A CENTURY AGO, the philosopher Friedrich Nietzsche painted a picture of the world as having no inherent meaning or purpose. The idea of God was a great deception, and traditional morality and religion were not just irrelevant, but an obstacle to power and progress. The future would belong to those courageous enough to create their own meaning. The winners would be known not for submission to a fanciful understanding of God, but through their becoming godlike in the quest for power.

The Nietzschean outlook on life is often called *nihilism*: the belief that life is meaningless, and religious and moral principles are unfounded. Christianity stands in direct contradiction. According to the Bible, life is purposeful, not meaningless. And it is not belief in God but the denial of his existence that is the great deception in our world today.

In the Scriptures, we see that this God (who is the ultimate reality—not simply the greatest of all beings but *Being* itself) is personal and relational. God is the maker and sustainer of all things. He is the Lord. God's creation and kingship extend not only to the visible things of this world but also to the invisible realm, including spiritual powers and authorities.

In a world that often lives as if there is no God, or as if God is whatever we imagine him to be, or as if God is just one of many potential deities, Christianity, like a comet streaking across the sky, declares the identity of the God who made us. The God we see revealed in Scripture is unique, the Great I AM. God gives us his name in a famous story near the beginning of the Bible, when God appears to Moses in a burning bush (Exodus 3). The name I AM implies that God is always present, active and involved, fully independent, self-sufficient, sovereign, inexhaustible and all-encompassing, eternal, all-powerful. Like a flame that never dies. A bush that never stops burning.

As you move through the Bible, the revelation of God grows brighter and clearer. The one true God, the Great I AM, is the Father, the Son, and the Spirit. Christians call this the Trinity—one God in three persons. It is the central tenet of all Christian theology, and we will return to it often in this catechism.

In the tortured vision of Nietzsche, the best life is found when we become a "superman"—not the caped hero of comic book fame but the ideal individual who succeeds at transcending conventional morality and societal norms to create our own values and purpose in life. In contrast, Christianity teaches that God is the source of the transcendence we long for. He is Life itself.

Nietzsche proclaimed the death of God, yet it is Nietzsche who died, while God still lives. In contrast to a nihilistic vision of the world that reduces all conflict to power and leads only to despair, Christianity claims the majestic, awe-inspiring, holy God of love exists as Father, Son, and Spirit, that self-giving love is the key to the mystery of life, and that all the goodness and happiness in the world can be traced back to the fountain of all joy, the divine dance of God at the center of all things.

REFLECTION QUESTIONS

1. **How does the Christian understanding of God as Father, Son, and Spirit provide a meaningful alternative to the perspective that life has no inherent purpose?** Reflect on how the relational nature of the Trinity (Father, Son, and Spirit) offers a framework for understanding purpose, meaning, and community in contrast to Nietzsche's view that God is a deception. How does this relational aspect of God shape your sense of purpose and identity?

2. **In what ways does acknowledging God as both Creator and King challenge the secular view that we must create our own meaning and purpose?** Consider how believing God as the ultimate authority and sustainer of all things shapes your understanding of reality. How does this belief influence your daily decisions, values, and sense of security compared to an outlook on life that denies divine authority?

3. **How can God's attributes provide comfort and guidance in your life?** Reflect on the significance of God's nature as infinite, eternal, and unchangeable in wisdom, power, holiness, justice, goodness, and truth. How do these attributes influence your trust in God, especially during challenging times?

SCRIPTURE REFERENCES

Scriptures on God as "I AM"

- Exodus 3:14
- Isaiah 41:4
  Isaiah 43:10
- John 8:58

Scriptures on God as Trinity

- Matthew 28:19
- John 1:1-3
  John 14:26
- 2 Corinthians 13:14

Scriptures on God as Creator and King

- Genesis 1:1
- Psalm 19:1
  Psalm 95:3
- Isaiah 40:28
- Colossians 1:16-17
- Revelation 4:11

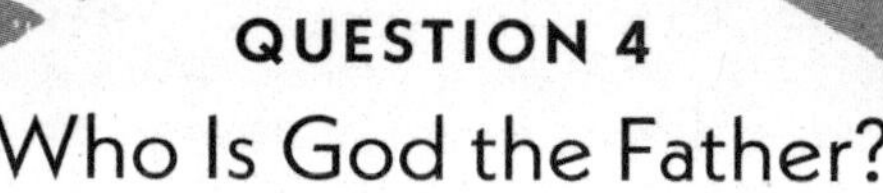

QUESTION 4

Who Is God the Father?

ANSWER

God the Father is the Almighty One, infinitely great and good, whose name is hallowed in heaven and on earth. He is not a distant authority, but a holy God filled with fatherly love.

THE IDEA OF GOD AS *Father* stirs up unpleasant thoughts for many people in our day. Some may remember the overbearing authority of their fathers, perhaps exerted in abusive ways. Others remember the absence of their fathers, or their fathers' indifference to what was good for the family. It's no wonder that some recommend we dispense with fatherly descriptors of God altogether.

But the Bible betrays no hint of embarrassment or reticence in describing God as Father. Even if we know God is spirit, thus transcending physical categories of male and female, and even if we can point to occasional motherly descriptors assigned to God in the biblical text, the overwhelming witness of Scripture is that God is our Father. Which means, rather than projecting all our experiences of earthly fathers onto God, as if he were merely a bigger and better version of whatever dad you had growing up (or the dad who was absent), we should see God as setting the standard for what fathering looks like. Some dads reflect him well. Others fail miserably. But *he* is the lens through which we assess what fatherhood should be, not the other way around.

The Bible describes the all-powerful nature of God as Father. "I believe in God the Father Almighty," says the ancient Apostles' Creed, "creator of heaven and earth." In calling God Father, the authors of the Bible reveal a God who is life-giving. Ancient theologians described the Trinity—the one God in three persons: Father, Son, and Spirit—in creative ways, sometimes speaking of the Father's eternal love for the Son through the Spirit. For our present purposes, it's sufficient to note how we benefit from the life-giving love of the Father, who for all eternity has never known a moment he didn't enjoy loving another or delighting in having another beside him.[1]

Many imagine God as a grumpy grandfather, a distant authority figure just waiting to catch us making a mistake. But the picture we see in Scripture is of a holy and happy God. He is infinitely great and good, yes. Majestic. Fiery. Set apart. We are to pray for his name to be hallowed—that's a beautiful older English word that means *honored* and *sanctified*—in all the earth. Yet, this same holy God sings over his children in love (Zephaniah 3:17). He delights in welcoming us into his love for his Son, so much that we too can call him *our* Father. In his attributes and his work, he reveals unfathomable kindness and grace.

The Old Testament describes the Father as gentle and compassionate toward those who fear him (Psalm 103:13). He gives wisdom and instruction that lead to life (Proverbs 4:1-2). He reproves those he loves like an earthly father should (Proverbs 3:12). The Bible tells us the Father knows what we need (Matthew 6:8), plans out our future (Psalm 139:16), and is ready to provide comfort for every pain (2 Corinthians 1:3). The love and devotion of earthly fathers, even the best, will be inconsistent. But God is perfect in his fatherly love. He is infinitely great and good.

REFLECTION QUESTIONS

1. **How does seeing God as holy and filled with fatherly love reshape your view of authority and power?** Reflect on how your past experiences with your father might influence your perception of God, both positively and negatively. How does the biblical portrayal of God the Father as infinitely great and good help you reconcile these views and trust his guidance and discipline?

2. **In what ways does acknowledging God the Father as both infinitely powerful and deeply personal shape your relationship**

with him? Consider how the combination of God's power and his closeness influences your approach to prayer, decision-making, and dealing with life's challenges. How does this understanding provide comfort and confidence in his plans for you?

3. **How can you reflect the traits of God the Father—his love, his joy, and his creative power—in your relationships and responsibilities?** What does a life of self-giving love, wisdom, and strength look like, as you interact with others? How can you be a source of support and guidance, modeling the character of God in your family, community, and work?

SCRIPTURE REFERENCES

- Deuteronomy 32:6
- Psalm 103:13
  Psalm 139:1-2
- Isaiah 64:8
- Matthew 6:9
  Matthew 7:11
- John 3:16
  John 13:3
- Romans 8:15
- 2 Corinthians 6:18
- Galatians 4:6-7
- James 1:17

QUESTION 5

Who Is God the Son?

ANSWER

God the Son is the eternal Word who took on humanity: Jesus of Nazareth, the Messiah of Israel and King of the world. He is not a life coach or therapist who affirms all our desires, but the Great Physician whose blood heals our sin-sick hearts.

EVERYONE WANTS JESUS ON THEIR side. That's why you often hear people say things like, "My Jesus would never" or describe "my Jesus" in ways that line up with whatever they already think. The world is full of manufactured ideas about Jesus. You can find just about any version of Jesus that suits you—a Jesus who cheers you on as you pursue all your hopes and dreams, a Jesus who will never challenge your choices, a Jesus who hates all the same people you hate, or a Jesus who blesses and affirms your life as you want it to be.

The most popular version of Jesus today casts him in the role of a life coach who is there to help you achieve your goals rather than someone who might call into question your goals or offer a new direction. Another version of Jesus casts him in the role of the therapist who affirms all our desires rather than someone who might challenge our feelings or offer to replace our selfish dreams with a new set of desires. Then there are versions of Jesus that cast him as a useful advocate for whatever cause or agenda we're most passionate about.

The four biographies of Jesus contained in the Bible (the Gospels) shatter all these mythical versions of Jesus. The Bible portrays Jesus as the Son of God, the eternal Word of God who is uncreated and has always existed (John 1:1). The Son took on humanity and came into the world as a historical person who grew up in the backwater town of Nazareth in Judea in the first century. His ministry marked him as the Messiah, a title that comes from the Hebrew word "anointed one." In his life and work, he fulfilled the ancient prophecies of Israel, taught about the kingdom of God, and claimed he was the chosen one bringing the long story of Israel to its rightful climax.

Jesus is more than a good teacher, a life coach, a therapist, or an advocate. The New Testament claims Jesus is King of the world. He has supreme authority. In future questions devoted in more detail to the life and ministry of Jesus, we will consider the significance of his death on the cross and his resurrection from the dead.

At the same time, this Jesus, named both Son of God and Son of Man, is a King marked by self-giving love, and the blood he spilled on the cross for us is for our healing. In the end, we don't need a coach; we need a Savior. We don't need an anesthetic; we need a surgeon. We don't need a heart tune-up; we need a heart transplant. The real Jesus is not a cheerleader for our feelings, but a doctor for our souls. The real Jesus isn't an advocate we get on our side. It's being on *his* side that matters.

REFLECTION QUESTIONS

1. **How do you reconcile the differing images of Jesus you encounter (cultural, personal, or religious) with the biblical portrait of Jesus as the eternal Word of God and King of the world?** Consider how the true Jesus, as described in Scripture, challenges or aligns with your previous notions or cultural representations of him. How can you ensure your understanding of Jesus is rooted in biblical truth?

2. **In what ways does understanding Jesus as the Great Physician, rather than just a life coach or a therapist, deepen your appreciation of his role in your life?** Reflect on the significance of Jesus's self-sacrifice and how it addresses not only the needs we feel, but the deeper needs we may be unaware of.

3. **How can recognizing Jesus as the Messiah of Israel in fulfillment of God's ancient plan help you learn to trust in his promises?** Reflect on the continuity of God's plan from the Old Testament to the New Testament and how Jesus fulfills the prophecies and expectations of the Messiah. How does this knowledge strengthen your faith and trust in God's overarching plan for your life?

SCRIPTURE REFERENCES

The Eternal Word

- John 1:1-3
- Colossians 1:15-17
- Hebrews 1:1-3

Jesus Taking on Humanity

- John 1:14
- Galatians 4:4-5
- Philippians 2:5-8

Jesus of Nazareth

- Matthew 2:23
- Mark 1:9
- John 1:45-46

The Messiah of Israel

- Isaiah 7:14
- Micah 5:2
- Zechariah 9:9
- John 1:41

King of the World

- Matthew 28:18
- 1 Timothy 6:15
- Revelation 19:16

Great Physician

- Mark 2:17
- Luke 5:31-32
- John 3:17

Self-Sacrificial Love

- John 10:18
- Philippians 2:5-8
- 1 John 3:16
  1 John 4:8-10

QUESTION 6

Who Is God the Spirit?

ANSWER

God the Spirit is the empowering presence of God in the world—the Lord, the giver of life. We are defined not by our inner self or spirituality, but by the Spirit's presence as he makes us new and blesses the world through our service in Jesus's name.

IT'S HARD TO FIND A more slippery term these days than *spirituality*. This word often refers to our personalized and subjective practices intended, in some way, to get in touch with transcendence or find something inside us that's "real." Phrases like "getting in touch with the universe" or "finding my truth" signal an individualistic approach to spirituality, as if there's an impersonal force or cosmic energy we can tap into. In earnest attempts to strengthen "our inner self," we turn to mindfulness apps, meditation practices, wellness rituals, or exercise routines that promise benefits for our personal wellbeing.

The rise of various spiritualities provides an excellent starting point for conversation about the nature of the world and the purpose of life, because these attempts at touching something transcendent indicate that this world is not all there is. We were made for something more. But looking to our inner self or our own spirituality does not bring ultimate satisfaction. The Bible directs us to look *upward* before we look *inward,* because, as we've seen, God is the center and point of everything. And the good news is, God the Spirit provides the power and presence we so desperately yearn for.

The Bible presents the Holy Spirit as God's personal and active presence in the lives of believers. It's common for people to think of the Spirit as a kind of energy or force, but the Scriptures describe the Spirit in personal terms. He guides, convicts, and empowers us. He can be grieved (Ephesians 4:30). The Spirit is available not to bring about personal enlightenment or to give us a "spiritual side," but to align our lives with God's purpose and standard. The Spirit prays through us and for us when we don't know what to pray (Romans 8:26-27). The Spirit reminds us what Jesus has taught (John 14:26).

The Nicene Creed (AD 381), which lays out a clear description of the Trinity—one God in three persons—describes the Holy Spirit as "the Lord, the giver of life." Not only was the Spirit active in the creation of the world, but he also brings about a new creation in the hearts and minds of those who follow Jesus—convicting us of wrongdoing, regenerating our hearts, and renewing our lives as we put off the old self and put on the new self (Ephesians 4:23).

In a world where people are attracted to all kinds of spiritual practices, the Bible reminds us of the importance of the Spirit in bringing about real and lasting life change. In the end, we are defined not by our futile attempts at finding ourselves or achieving some kind of super-spiritual status, but by the Spirit's presence in us. By the Spirit's power we are made new. By the Spirit's power we bring blessing to the world. By the Spirit's power we serve others in Jesus's name.

This is the glory of the Trinity, the central tenet of the Christian faith: the Father, the Son, and the Spirit are one God, the same in substance, equal in power and glory.[1]

REFLECTION QUESTIONS

1. **How does recognizing the Holy Spirit as the empowering presence of God in your life influence your daily actions and decisions?** Reflect on how acknowledging the presence and guidance of the Holy Spirit can change how you approach your daily tasks, challenges, and interactions. How can you more deeply depend on the Spirit's power and leading in your everyday life?

2. **In what ways has the Holy Spirit transformed your understanding of your identity and purpose?** Consider how the Spirit's work has redefined who you are and what you are called to do. How does

the Spirit's indwelling presence shape your sense of self and your mission in the world?

3. **How can you actively participate in blessing the world through the love and good works empowered by the Holy Spirit?** Reflect on specific ways you can be an ambassador of Jesus the King, bringing the presence and power of the Holy Spirit to those around you. How can you use the gifts and guidance of the Spirit to serve others and share God's love more effectively?

SCRIPTURE REFERENCES

- Matthew 28:19
- Luke 1:31, 35
- John 14:16-17, 26
  John 15:26
  John 16:13
  John 17:25-26
- Acts 1:8
  Acts 2:4
  Acts 10:47-48
- Romans 5:5
  Romans 8:9
  Romans 8:26-27
- 1 Corinthians 12:4-7
- 2 Corinthians 13:14
- Ephesians 1:13-14
- 1 Thessalonians 1:6
- Titus 3:5-6

PART 2

Creation and Identity

God created the world out of his sovereign will and love, displaying his glory, creativity, and goodness in every aspect of creation. The universe reflects his nature and character in all its complexity and beauty. The world's catechism has many theories for who we are, where we come from, and what life is about. In the sections ahead, we'll consider some of these elements with respect to the environment, sexuality, work, and rest. The Bible presents a story that connects with and confronts the world's story. This section of the catechism will tell that story for us.

God created humans in his image and likeness, giving us a unique identity and purpose. We are designed to know, love, and glorify him, finding our ultimate fulfillment in a relationship with our Creator. Our identity is rooted in being his image-bearers, reflecting his attributes, and engaging in meaningful relationships with others. Sexuality is a significant aspect of our identity, designed by God for procreation, unity, and intimacy within the covenant of marriage between a man and a woman. It reflects the relational aspect of God's nature and his design for human flourishing.

We are called to steward God's creation, exercising dominion and responsibility over the earth. This involves caring for the environment, using resources wisely, and promoting justice and peace. Work is a gift from God, allowing us to participate in his creative and sustaining activities. It is a means of serving others, developing our talents, and glorifying God. Rest is equally important. It reminds us of our dependence on God and his provision. It is a time for renewal, reflection, and worship, acknowledging that our worth is not based on our productivity.

Freedom is not about independent living but about being liberated from sin to live according to God's design and purpose. True freedom is found in surrendering to God's will and experiencing his abundant life. Understanding creation and identity enables us to discover the unique strands of our purpose, value, and the rich tapestry of life that God intends for us.

QUESTION 7

Why Did God Create the World?

ANSWER

God created everything by his Word, not because he was lonely, but out of the free overflow of divine love, so that all creation would enjoy his glory.

"THE COSMOS IS WITHIN US," Carl Sagan said in a famous book and documentary.[1] "We are made of star stuff. We are a way for the universe to know itself."[2] Sagan's words capture a prevalent cultural narrative that leans on a naturalistic understanding of the universe's origins. In previous eras, some scientists say, there were gaps in human knowledge about the universe, so naturally, people attributed whatever they didn't or couldn't understand to the divine intervention of God. Today, however, those gaps in human knowledge are shrinking. There are fewer and fewer reasons to rely on a "god of the gaps."[3] The more science explains, the less necessary God becomes.

A naturalistic understanding of the world sounds plausible to many today, but if matter is all there is, and if everything about the world is predetermined or can be attributed to merely natural causes, the universal human desire for meaning, significance, and a life beyond this world must be wrongheaded. It's a mirage. We long for something that isn't there. Some who deny the existence of God say, *That's right, so grow up and come to terms with the stark reality that there is no ultimate purpose in life, other than the meaning and significance you establish for yourself!*

In contrast to this way of seeing the world, the Bible begins with a different presupposition: there is a God who created everything. This is a foundational truth of Christianity. The reason most people throughout history have believed and most people around the world today continue to believe in a transcendent being responsible for creating the world is not due to a lack of education or scientific expertise, but because God is really there.

Some who do believe in God might think he created the world because he was bored or lonely, as if he needed companionship. But as we've seen in the section on who God is, nothing could be further from the truth. God wasn't lonely; God was eternally happy as Father, Son, and Spirit. God wasn't compelled to make the world; he did so out of the free overflow of his Trinitarian love. We are created by God to find joy in his eternal glory. God made us for *God*.

What's more, the Bible teaches that God created the world through the power of his Word (Genesis 1:1-3). God created all that is, from nothing—he didn't use preexisting raw materials. He spoke, and the universe came into existence (Psalm 33:6-9). God is the source of everything that is, the ultimate reason there is something rather than nothing.

The reality of God as Creator provides a framework that gives our life meaning, purpose, and direction. We were made for God. Creation is the theater of his glory. The God who has revealed himself owns all he has made. His design is what matters. His purpose is what stands. According to Scripture, we don't make meaning or purpose for ourselves; we discover meaning and purpose in line with God's design.

REFLECTION QUESTIONS

1. **How does understanding that God created the world out of the free overflow of divine love, rather than out of necessity or loneliness, shape your view of his character and your relationship with him?** Reflect on how this understanding influences your perception of God's nature and his intentions toward creation. How does it affect your trust and worship of him?

2. **In what ways does acknowledging that all creation intends to bring glory to God change your perspective on your purpose and daily activities?** Consider how the purpose of glorifying God can be integrated into your everyday life, from your work and relationships to your personal goals and hobbies. How can this perspective guide your actions and decisions?

3. **How do the concepts of God's ownership and sovereignty over creation impact your attitude toward the world and your responsibilities?** Reflect on the implications of God being the Creator and owner of everything. How does this influence your stewardship of resources and treatment of others?

SCRIPTURE REFERENCES

- Genesis 1:1
- Exodus 20:11
- Psalm 19:1
  Psalm 95:3
- Isaiah 40:28
- Jeremiah 10:10-12
- John 1:1-3, 11
- Ephesians 1:4-5
- Colossians 1:16-17
  Colossians 3:10
- Revelation 4:11

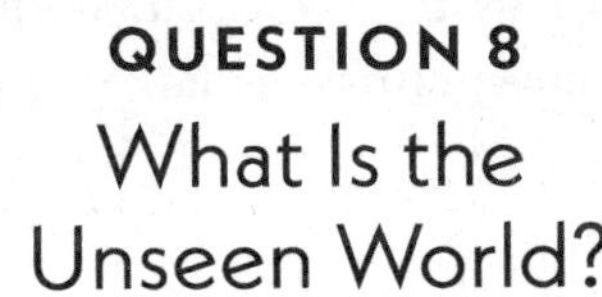

QUESTION 8

What Is the Unseen World?

ANSWER

The physical world is not all there is. The Bible describes an unseen realm of spiritual realities, with angels and demons engaged in cosmic struggle over God's plan of redemption.

BEFORE WE CONTINUE OUR EXPLORATION of God's work in creation, we need to address a vitally important aspect of the Bible's vision of reality. In the Western world today, many assume the physical world is all there is; we focus attention on whatever is provable through science. We imagine a world without God or the supernatural.

Most people who live outside of Western culture (and most people who have lived throughout history) see the world differently. In most places on earth, it's taken for granted that there is an unseen realm, where spiritual realities invisible to us exist and have real power. The Bible lines up with this way of thinking, not the Western outlook that reduces everything to matter. In the Bible's description of the world, we find a supernatural dimension filled with spiritual forces, where the cosmic struggle between angels and fallen angels (demons) unfolds as part of God's plan of redemption.

As much as we'd like to have more detail, the Bible doesn't give us a clear and specific account of when, why, or how this spiritual realm was brought into existence, or why certain angels rebelled against God, or just how prevalent and powerful these forces are in our day-to-day lives. What *is* clear in Scripture is that this unseen world includes angels and demons—active participants in the cosmic narrative.

The Bible teaches that reality extends beyond what can be seen, touched, or quantified. Christians walk by faith, not by sight (2 Corinthians 5:7). Supernatural elements of existence cannot be fully explained by science; there is more than meets the eye or can be tested in a laboratory.

In our culture today, it's common to scoff at supernatural explanations for what happens in our world. Yet the Bible remains a treasury of insights into a hidden spiritual world, countering secular perspectives. Even the church demonstrates unseen supernatural power. Ephesians 3:10 explains that the church unveils God's wisdom to spiritual authorities in heavenly realms!

The Bible describes a cosmic struggle between angels and demons over God's plan of redemption. Ephesians 6:12 speaks of "spiritual forces of evil in the heavens," affirming that unseen entities engage in spiritual conflict. Daniel 10:12-13 depicts angelic beings in cosmic struggles impacting human life. Supernatural forces work behind our everyday experiences.

Chief among fallen angels is Satan, often called "the Accuser" or "the Evil One." Although his power is never described as being on par with God's, the Bible is clear that Satan is active. He is depicted as a prowling lion seeking to devour and destroy (1 Peter 5:8). In the early church, when new believers were baptized, candidates would renounce Satan and his works. Jesus taught his followers to pray, "Deliver us from the evil one" (Matthew 6:13).

We can wave all this away as if it's mere superstition, but the unseen realm is integral to the biblical view of reality. The Bible asserts the presence and influence of supernatural forces on human history. If we are to enter and inhabit the Bible's story, we must allow the Scriptures to challenge our tendency to ignore or minimize the reality of the unseen realm of angels and demons.

REFLECTION QUESTIONS

1. **How does the idea that the physical world is not all there is challenge or align with your beliefs about reality?** Discuss how this perspective affects your understanding of life, the universe, and your place within it. Consider both the intellectual and practical implications of acknowledging an unseen realm.

2. **In what ways does recognizing the existence of angels and demons provide a richer understanding of God's plan of redemption?** Explore how the concept of a cosmic struggle between good and evil influences your perception of spiritual warfare and redemption.

3. **How might acknowledging the unseen spiritual world influence your daily life and decisions?** Reflect on how an awareness of spiritual realities might shape your actions, choices, and outlook. Consider practical steps to remain mindful of the spiritual dimension in your everyday life.

SCRIPTURE REFERENCES

- Genesis 3:15
- Psalm 82:1
  Psalm 91:11-12
- Isaiah 66:16
- Daniel 10:13
- Matthew 18:10
  Matthew 28:1-3, 18-20
- 2 Corinthians 4:18
- Ephesians 6:12
- Colossians 1:16
- Hebrews 1:14
  Hebrews 11:3
- 1 Peter 5:8
- Revelation 12:7-9

QUESTION 9
Why Did God Create Us?

ANSWER

God created us in his image, to know and love him and share his joy. The good life is found not in inventing our purpose but in bowing to God's design and reflecting his glory.

ACCORDING TO THE PHILOSOPHER Michael Allan Gillespie, "One strain of Enlightenment thought...came to believe that humans were gods, the other strain saw them as beasts or even mere matter in motion, driven by desire and sheer self-interest."[1] This statement captures the two poles in secular thought about human identity. At one end, we tend to elevate humanity to godlike status, believing in our limitless potential. At the other, we reduce humans to biological entities driven by primal instincts and material desires. Neither of these extreme views produces a satisfying way of life.

These two poles lead to confusion and create a crisis of meaning. If humans are gods, self-creation and autonomy are paramount; we rise in pride but then deflate into despair when we cannot meet our own expectations. If humans are mere animals, there is no inherent purpose to life; we just make things up as we go.

The Bible paints a different picture. We are not autonomous individuals, creating ourselves constantly by our decisions and choices; we are images, we are reflections. The dignity of our humanity is derivative; it comes from him whose image we bear. We have worth and value not because of anything in ourselves, but because we are created in the image of God. We are not mere creatures; because we bear the image of God, we are in some sense godlike. But we are not God; because we are created, we are still creatures.

According to Scripture, we are created in God's image with a purpose: to know him, to love him, and to share his joy. God made us for relationship. He wants to be known. He wants us to experience—in him—the joy of all we were made to be.

Being made in God's image, we reflect his attributes. We stand apart from other creatures in our relationality, rationality, creativity, and authority. And regardless of our abilities or achievements, our ethnicity or gender, we believe every human has inherent worth because we all bear God's image.

Why does knowing and loving God bring joy? Because this is what we were created for. Our hearts were made for this relationship. This joy is not dependent on our circumstances or external factors but is rooted in our relationship with God and the eternal hope we have in him.

In contrast to the common sense of the world, we do not look inside to discover and define ourselves. No, we look up to God; we find in his good design our purpose, and in reflecting his character we find fullness of joy. When we try to create a purpose for our lives apart from God, we fall short of God's glory. Any attempt at independence or self-definition will leave us empty and unsatisfied. Bowing to God's purpose for our lives is the prerequisite for living the good life he intends for us.

REFLECTION QUESTIONS

1. **How does the truth about being made in God's image shape your self-understanding and purpose?** Reflect on how this understanding affects your sense of self-worth and your approach to life's purpose. How does it shape your view of your abilities, achievements, and interactions with others?

2. **What are some practices that can help you better align your life with the pursuit of joy in knowing and loving God, rather than inventing your purpose?** Consider the areas where you might seek fulfillment outside your relationship with God. How can you

reorient these aspects to find more profound satisfaction and align them with God's design and purpose for you?

3. **What are some implications of everyone being made in the image of God?** How does our understanding of the image of God in humanity strike against racial injustice? How does the dignity of all image-bearers influence how we treat those less fortunate than us?

SCRIPTURE REFERENCES

- Genesis 1:26-28
- Psalm 16:11
  Psalm 100:3
  Psalm 139:13-14
- Proverbs 3:5-6
- Isaiah 43:7
- Micah 6:8
- John 15:11
- 1 Corinthians 10:31
- Ephesians 2:10
- Colossians 1:16
  Colossians 3:10
- Revelation 4:11

QUESTION 10

Who Are We?

ANSWER

We are persons beloved by God, created to love God, love others, and care for the world he has made. We become like what we love. Our identity is found not by looking within ourselves but looking up to God.

WHO ARE YOU? IT'S ONE of the most important and profound questions anyone can ask.

In today's world, it's common to think you'd answer this question by looking deep inside yourself, discovering your dreams and desires, and then expressing your unique essence to the world. "Be yourself," we say—over against the past, society in the present, religious commitments, family expectations, or political party. The modern heroes are true to themselves no matter what anyone else thinks.

The Bible paints a different picture. First and foremost, we are beloved. Ponder this for a moment: the God who created us loves us. And this loving Creator has given us a purpose: to love him, to love others, and care for the world he has made. According to Scripture, we do not discover who we are by looking within. We need someone—God—to tell us who we are. We need a voice from the outside to affirm our value. Living without this identity-shaping voice sends us to all sorts of imitations to figure out who we are.

The world says to find yourself, look within yourself and then follow your heart. But Jesus taught that true life is found in losing oneself, in denying yourself and following *him* (Matthew 10:39). According to Jesus, identity is not found by looking inward but by looking up to God and seeking his will for our lives.

Once we look up, we realize that our identity is not self-created, but is rooted in God's love and purpose for us. From the beginning of the Bible, we see that humanity was created in God's image and given the mandate to care for the world (Genesis 1:26-28). Every person has inherent dignity and worth as a beloved creation of God and is called to use their gifts and abilities to serve him and others.

Furthermore, our hearts and minds are shaped by the things we love and value. We become like what we worship. Jesus taught that "where your treasure is, there your heart will be also" (Matthew 6:21). Proverbs 4:23 says to guard our hearts, for everything you do flows from them. The apostle Paul urged the Colossians to set their minds on things above, not earthly things (Colossians 3:2). Our desires and affections profoundly impact who we are and who we become.

Christianity holds that our identity is not something we invent or discover on our own, but something given us by our Creator. Our identity is not based on our self-perception or the opinions of others but on the fact that we are loved and valued by God as his children. This means our truest identity is not found within ourselves but by looking up to God, who created us for a purpose and has a plan for our lives. As we seek to know him more deeply and love what he loves, we discover who we are and find fulfillment in the unique role he has for us to play in the world he has made.

REFLECTION QUESTIONS

1. **In what ways have you sought to define your identity by looking inside to your desires? What does it look like for you to find your identity in God's love and purpose for you?** Reflect on specific instances where you have tried to find your worth and identity by looking inward.

2. **How do your current commitments reflect your love for God, your love for others, and your responsibility to care for the world?** Examine your roles and responsibilities and how they align with

God's design for humanity. Identify areas where your heart may need to be redirected to reflect God's love more fully.

3. **What steps can you take to better align your understanding with the biblical view that your identity is given by God and not self-created?** Consider practical actions you can implement daily to shift your focus from self-discovery to seeking God's will. This might include prayer, studying Scripture, going to church, community service, or fostering relationships that encourage mutual growth in faith.

SCRIPTURE REFERENCES

- Genesis 1:26-27
- Psalm 139:13-14
- Micah 6:8
- Matthew 5:44
  Matthew 22:37-39
- Mark 12:28-34
- Romans 8:14-15
- 1 Corinthians 10:31
- Ephesians 2:10
- Philippians 2:1-11
- Colossians 3:23-34
- 1 John 3:1-2
  1 John 4:19

QUESTION 11

What Is Sexuality?

ANSWER

Sexuality is a God-given aspect of humanity. Male and female, our bodies are designed for procreation through the union of a man and woman in marriage. Sexuality is embodied, not imagined; physically grounded, not psychologically determined.

"**NATURE MADE A MISTAKE,** which I have corrected."[1] These are the words of Christine Jorgensen, one of the first people to undergo sex reassignment surgery, claiming that nature was wrong in placing "her true self" in a man's body. It's common today for people to think the body doesn't determine our identity or self-perception. "Who I feel I am inside" is all that matters in discerning the meaning of the human body. Likewise, it's common for sexual activity to be recast in terms of self-expression and personal pleasure, detached from any inherent design or moral framework. Our sexual attractions become authoritative, constituting the core of our identity. Not surprisingly, marriage has been mangled into something malleable, a contract dignifying the sexual desires of consenting adults, severed from the idea that marriage brings together the two halves of humanity with the intent of bringing new life into the world.

Perhaps nowhere does Christianity's vision of humanity and the body come into sharper conflict with the world today than in questions surrounding sexuality and marriage. All throughout the Bible—from the first chapters of Genesis, to the teaching of Jesus, to the cosmic marriage feast in Revelation—we see that our creation in the image of God, as male and female, is an unmistakable element of God's good design.

Our bodies are integral to our identity. Christians believe in the goodness of the body, even when our bodies let us down, or we sense discomfort with how God made us, or when our bodies don't work properly. Bodily existence is *good.* And the body *means* something. Differences between men and women are not merely socially constructed; they are rooted in bodily realities.

Christians believe our bodies are not just physical vessels but are temples of the Holy Spirit (1 Corinthians 6:19-20). That's why God values our bodies and instructs us on how to live as embodied people. The Spirit of God indwells his people, and God calls us to treat the body he made as holy, sacred, and set apart (1 Corinthians 3:16-17).

Likewise, sexual intimacy is not just a physical act; it is a spiritual and emotional bond intended for marriage. This bond reflects the covenantal nature of marriage and is ordered toward procreation and the continuation of human life. It also reflects the complementary nature of male and female, forming a family unit that aligns with God's design for human flourishing. The Bible also places a high value on those who, temporarily or all their life, remain unmarried (1 Corinthians 7; Revelation 14:4). Singleness and marriage show, in different ways, the union between Christ and his people.

In a world marred by sexual confusion, Christianity brings good news. The church issues the most inclusive invitation in human history, welcoming people from every background, no matter their self-perception or struggle. At the same time, this invitation is transformative, offering a life-changing relationship with God that redeems and refines our understanding of identity and sexuality. The Bible upholds a view of sexuality as a God-given gift designed for expression within the covenant of marriage between a man and woman. This teaching reflects God's original design for humanity, and Christians believe true human flourishing comes from living according to his wisdom and love.

REFLECTION QUESTIONS

1. **How does understanding sexuality as a God-given aspect of humanity shape the way you think about people being made male and female?** Reflect on the meaning and significance of being created as sexed beings—male and female—and what God's design tells us about his purpose for our bodies.

2. **In what ways have cultural narratives around sexuality and gender influenced your beliefs and behaviors?** Examine the cultural messages you encounter regarding sexual freedom, gender fluidity, and sexual autonomy. Reflect on how these narratives may have shaped your views and where you need a deeper understanding of the Bible's view of sexuality.

3. **How can you embody a biblical vision of sexuality marked by humility, grace, and compassion?** Consider practical ways to live out and share the biblical perspective on sexuality, especially in a world that often holds opposing views. How can you approach sensitive conversations and relationships with love and understanding while maintaining your convictions?

SCRIPTURE REFERENCES

- Genesis 1:27-28
  Genesis 2:18-24
- Leviticus 18:22
- Matthew 19:4-6
- Romans 1:18-32
- 1 Corinthians 6:18-20
  1 Corinthians 7:1-9
- Galatians 5:19-21
- Ephesians 5:31-33
- Colossians 3:5-10
- 1 Thessalonians 4:3-7
- Hebrews 13:4

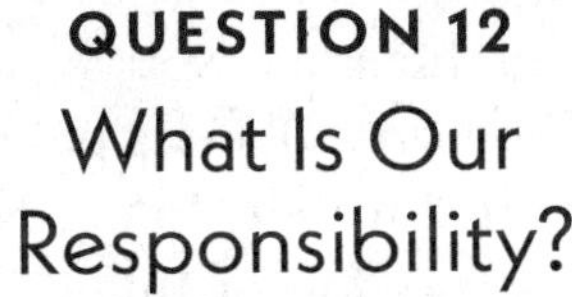

QUESTION 12

What Is Our Responsibility?

ANSWER

Our responsibility is to represent God by ruling wisely over his good creation, exercising authority in life-giving ways. We are called not to abandon or abuse our authority, but to serve as stewards.

THE CONCEPT OF "RESPONSIBILITY" has fallen on hard times. A smattering of misuses and abuses of power, authority, and responsibility are found all over the news. You don't have to search hard to find leaders taking advantage of their entrusted authority and exploiting others for selfish purposes. Every sphere of reality contains degrees of abuse—from the halls of governments to multinational corporations to the organized religions of our day.

In the Western world, we often have a built-in bias against the idea of authority. We see responsibility or authority as bad, or at best, necessary evils. The ideal world would be one without hierarchy, where power is equally shared, where we'd try to minimize authority. Many of our cultural heroes rebel against institutions or authority in one way or another.

The Bible both lines up with and subverts this antiauthoritarian impulse. The Scriptures regularly condemn abuses and misuses of authority and unfulfilled responsibilities that lead to oppression. The power-hungry will be judged. At the same time, the Bible does not view power and authority as inherently wrong or just a necessary evil. On the contrary, the Bible sees both responsibility and authority as good and necessary for human flourishing.

When appropriately exercised and not in an authoritarian fashion, taking responsibility in the workplace ought to make things better for people, not worse. When everyone understands their role, taking responsibility in the home should contribute to everyone's wellbeing. A parent who exercises authority isn't doing something wrong but something right. That's what it means to be a parent. When things are working correctly, responsibility in government is not just a necessary evil but a positive force for good.

Human beings were created to rule. In our fallenness, that calling has been squandered. But that vocation of ruling wisely over the earth can be restored because of Jesus, the one who did for us what we failed to do for ourselves, the one who came to rule the way God always intended. Whenever we sing about Jesus as our Lord and our King, we are saying, *This is the one who fulfills God's original design for humanity. This is the one who rules wisely over this world. This is the one to whom our knees bow. Our tongues confess he is Lord.*

The King we worship chose a wooden cross for his throne. He came not to be served but to serve and to give his life as a ransom for many (Matthew 20:28). That's the kind of servant leadership that Jesus exercised. He is both the Suffering Servant and the conquering King. He is the Servant King. And in that paradox, we see the glory of what God always intended for his people—that we would lead, serve, rule, submit, subdue, and cultivate—in life-giving ways for those around us, and as a reflection of our good and loving God. Because of the cross and resurrection of Jesus, we have the promise of new life and the restoration of our original purpose.

REFLECTION QUESTIONS

1. **In what ways have you experienced the effects of people misusing their authority or abandoning the responsibility they should have taken?** Both the abuse of authority and the abandonment of authority lead to oppression. Consider times you've experienced authority gone bad.

2. **In what spheres of life have you been given responsibility for exercising authority wisely?** Consider the difference in being a good or bad steward of the resources and responsibility you've been given. When have you failed? When have you succeeded?

3. **How does Jesus's role as both servant and King alter worldly understandings of authority and responsibility?** In what ways can we reclaim authority as a good thing? How is the worldly exercise of power challenged by Jesus's example?

SCRIPTURE REFERENCES

- Genesis 1:26-28
  Genesis 2:15
- Psalm 8:6-8
  Psalm 103:19
- Matthew 25:21
  Matthew 28:18
- Luke 12:42-43
- Romans 13:1
- Ephesians 1:21-22
- Colossians 1:16-17
  Colossians 3:23-24
- 1 Peter 4:10

QUESTION 13
What Is Work?

ANSWER

Work is the gracious expression of creative energy in response to God's calling. We are to cultivate the world for the glory of God, offering our skills to serve our neighbors.

COMMON VIEWS OF WORK TODAY are often shaped by two competing influences. On the one side, many view work as a necessary evil, something we endure as a means to an end, such as financial stability or personal fulfillment. On the other side, many base their worth and value in their productivity and efficiency in work. Our identity gets enmeshed with whatever we do for a living and how good we are at doing it.

The Bible's vision of work redirects these influences. First, work is not a necessary evil. It's true that work can be toilsome and difficult in a fallen world, but from the beginning it's clear humans were made for work. In Genesis 1:28, God blessed Adam and Eve and then gave instruction about cultivating the earth. In Genesis 2:15, God placed Adam in the garden of Eden to work it and keep it. Thus, work is not a result of brokenness in the world but is part of God's intended purpose for humanity. When we work, we respond to God's good calling.

The New Testament goes further, teaching that all our work should be done to glorify God and serve others. "Whatever you do, do it from the heart, as something done for the Lord and not for people, knowing that you will receive the reward of an inheritance from the Lord. You serve the Lord Christ" (Colossians 3:23-24). So work is not merely a way to earn a living but an opportunity to serve and honor God by using our talents and skills to benefit others.

Second, the Bible warns us from basing our identity in our efficiency and productivity in how fruitful we are in our work. God's blessing comes first. We find our ultimate identity in being beloved by God, and therefore, when we work, we do so *from* a position of blessing (God blessed Adam and Eve before he gave them his command), not *for* a blessing. We have worth and value no matter what our work status is.

Cultivating the world for God's glory is rooted in the biblical concept of stewardship. God has entrusted us with the care of his creation, and we are to use our work to honor him and benefit others. Work is creative. We reflect God whenever we use our talents, skills, and resources to bring out the potential of creation and make the world a better place.

What's more, all work has dignity and value in God's eyes. Whether we are engaged in paid employment or unpaid work, whether we are professionals or laborers, whether we are working in the home or outside of it, our work is an opportunity to glorify God and serve others.

According to Scripture, work is not just a way to earn a living or achieve personal fulfillment but an opportunity to serve others and glorify God. We use our skills and resources to benefit our neighbors. In contrast to ways of thinking about work that prioritize individualism and self-interest, Christianity envisions work as a way of reflecting God and serving our neighbors.

REFLECTION QUESTIONS

1. **Are you more prone to see work as a necessary evil or to base your identity in your work?** Reflect on whether you see your work as a gift and calling from God or merely as a means to an end, or the source of your worth and value.

2. **How can you cultivate your work environment to reflect God's glory and serve your neighbors?** Think about practical steps to use your skills and resources to benefit others. Reflect on how you can promote justice, mercy, and compassion in your work, and how

you can make something in the world in the sphere God has called you.

3. **In what ways can you turn your work into worship?** Reflect on how you can reorient your perspective so you view your work as an act of devotion to God, intended for his glory.

SCRIPTURE REFERENCES

- Genesis 2:15
- Psalm 90:17
  Psalm 145
- Proverbs 12:11
  Proverbs 14:23
  Proverbs 16:3
- Ecclesiastes 3:12-13
  Ecclesiastes 9:10
- Matthew 5:16
- 1 Corinthians 10:31
- Galatians 6:9
- Ephesians 2:10
- Colossians 3:23-24
- 1 Thessalonians 4:11-12
- 1 Timothy 6:18

QUESTION 14
What Is Rest?

ANSWER

Rest is when we cease from striving. Our hearts are restless until they rest in God our Savior and Sustainer. Living his way renews us physically and spiritually, and provides a foretaste of eternal peace.

IT SEEMS AS IF EVERYONE wants a break these days, some way of finding rest in a supercharged world of frenetic activity. Our obsession with screens, diversions, distractions, and our demand for variety in food, drink, and apparel often leave us uneasy. From pot to propranolol, psychic practices, Prozac, and pinot grigio, we are trying to cope. For many, rest is reduced to the absence of activity or a break from work. For some, rest is viewed as a commodity to be consumed rather than a state of being to be cultivated. For others, the word implies laziness, idleness, and pursuing pleasure at all costs. At the end of all our work and all our rest, there remains a deep restlessness in the human heart.

Christianity provides a deeper and richer understanding of rest—a patterned dependence on God that leads us to cease from striving. Rest goes deeper than taking time off from work; it is about orienting our lives around God's will and finding our ultimate rest and fulfillment in him. In a culture that values busyness and productivity, we are called to rest in God our Savior and Sustainer, allowing him to renew us physically and spiritually.

In the first book of the Bible, God himself models rest. God rested on the seventh day after creating the universe (Genesis 2:2). This is significant because it shows us that resting is one of the ways we reflect God. He created us with the need for rest and has provided us with opportunities to demonstrate our dependence on him.

As the Bible's storyline unfolds, we increasingly see rest as a form of worship. The Sabbath was set apart for worship and rest in the presence of God (Exodus 20:8-11), a weekly reminder of God's goodness, faithfulness, and provision. Rest is also a means of renewal. Jesus invites all those who are weary and burdened to come to him for rest (Matthew 11:28-29). He holds out to us a life characterized by his Way. Rest is not only a temporary break from the demands of life, but also a deep and abiding peace that comes from being in relationship with Jesus.

In today's world, practicing rest is countercultural. Our vision of rest is rooted in God and points forward to the future. We believe we will one day rest in the peace God has prepared for his people (Revelation 21:1-4). And even now, we can experience a deep and abiding peace that transcends our present circumstances and points us toward the ultimate rest and peace that is promised us. Our current experience of rest is a foretaste of this future reality as we find temporary respite from the burdens of life in the presence of God. Resting is a radical act of resistance, a practice that sets us apart from the world and reminds us that our worth comes not from our productivity but from the blessing of God.

REFLECTION QUESTIONS

1. **What common ideas about rest most resonate with you? How can you align your understanding of rest with a biblical vision that emphasizes your dependence on God?** Reflect on how you perceive rest in your daily life. Consider whether you see it as mere escapism, productivity, self-care, or a luxury, and how these views compare to the biblical understanding of rest.

2. **What parts of your life are marked by an experience of restlessness?** Identify areas where you feel restless or uneasy. Contemplate what these areas of angst tell you about your life—your hopes and dreams and desires.

3. **What practices of rest can help you increase your dependence on God and reorient your heart to his purposes?** Consider practical steps you can take to align your life with God's rhythm of work and rest. What changes could you make to ensure your rest contains both physical and spiritual elements intended to deepen your relationship with God?

SCRIPTURE REFERENCES

- Genesis 2:2-3
- Exodus 20:8-11
- Psalm 4:8
  Psalm 23:1-3
  Psalm 62:1
- Isaiah 40:29-31
- Jeremiah 6:16
- Matthew 11:28-30
- Mark 6:31
- Philippians 4:6-7
- Hebrews 4:3, 9-11
- Revelation 14:13

QUESTION 15

What Is Freedom?

ANSWER

True freedom is submission to God. Freedom is not casting off all restraints and pursuing whatever we want. It is embracing the right restraints and aligning our wants with God's will, so we can pursue what is true and good and beautiful.

IN TODAY'S WORLD, FREEDOM IS often associated with individual autonomy and the ability to make choices free from external coercion or influence. Americans, more than most, value freedom and choice. The phones in our pockets allow us to access thousands of choices with our fingertips. We are engulfed in a cauldron of competing desires, trying to decide what we want.

An older view of freedom, what we might call "positive freedom," focused on the freedom to pursue some good aim. But today's idea of freedom has morphed into something we might call "negative freedom"—the absence of all outside constraints, influences, and forces. The modern understanding of freedom sounds enticing, but it is actually a form of slavery.

The problem with today's vision of freedom is that it doesn't work. No relationship can grow unless each person sacrifices some liberty to serve the other. In friendship, we set aside certain freedoms whenever someone else's needs impinge upon our time. In marriage, we give up a measure of freedom and independence in fidelity to our spouse. In parenting, we give up the freedom to do whatever we please so we can serve and support our kids. True freedom always involves surrendering lesser freedoms, trading one set of constraints for another, and submitting to new limitations. Freedom is about embracing the right limitations that lead to a fullness of life.

In today's world, instead of being bound by outside constraints, we become slaves to our internal desires. This is where the Bible's vision of freedom stands out. True freedom is not found in following our desires and impulses but aligning ourselves with God's will and pursuing the good he intends for us.

True freedom is not merely freedom *from* constraints, but freedom *for* something. When God set his people Israel free from slavery in Egypt, his purpose was that they would worship him in the desert. They were freed *from* captivity *for* worship. Freed *from* slavery to Pharoah *for* service to God.

The theme of freedom runs through the whole Bible. Our ultimate bondage is our rebellion against the God who made us. When Jesus preached his first sermon (Luke 4:16-21), he declared himself the long-promised Liberator. "[The Lord] has sent me...to set free the oppressed, to proclaim the year of the Lord's favor" (Luke 4:18-19). Bringing this rescue required Jesus to give up his life. He submitted to death as a slave so those who are slaves to wrongdoing might live his life of freedom. In the New Testament, when the apostle Paul wrote about how Christ set us free from the law, his focus was on what we are freed *for:* not a license to do wrong, but to live according to the Spirit and to follow God's will (Galatians 5:13-25).

True freedom isn't about doing whatever you want. It's about wanting what is true and good and beautiful and then pointing your life in that direction, choosing the right constraints as you walk in the freedom supplied by Jesus.

REFLECTION QUESTIONS

1. **In what areas of your life are you prone to pursue negative freedom (freedom *from* all constraints) instead of positive freedom (freedom *for* what is true, good, and beautiful)?** Reflect on how today's understanding of freedom as the absence of constraints has shaped your actions and mindset. Consider how this vision might have led to isolation or self-centeredness and how it contrasts with the biblical vision of freedom.

2. **What are some right restraints in your life that might help you align your wants with God's will?** Identify beneficial boundaries and constraints that guide you toward God's will. Think about how you can embrace and appreciate these constraints more intentionally as pathways to true freedom.

3. **How can you shift your understanding of freedom from pursuing your desires to pursuing what is true and good in alignment with God's will?** Consider practical steps to align your pursuits with God's desires. Reflect on how this shift can lead to a more profound sense of true freedom and fulfillment, moving beyond personal autonomy to a life of meaningful service and obedience to God.

SCRIPTURE REFERENCES

- Proverbs 3:5-6
- John 8:31-32
- Romans 6:18
  Romans 8:2
  Romans 12:1-2
- 2 Corinthians 3:17
- Galatians 5:1, 13-14, 16
- Philippians 4:8
- James 1:25
  James 4:7
- 1 Peter 2:16

PART 3

Fall and Sin

The biblical narrative addresses the reality of profound brokenness that now marks God's good creation. What has gone wrong lies in humanity's rebellion against God. This rebellion began with Adam and Eve's disobedience in the garden of Eden, bringing sin and death into the world. As a result, the perfect harmony between God, humanity, and creation was shattered.

Our sin against God is characterized by idolatry and self-centeredness. We turn away from God's authority and seek to live independently, placing our desires above his commands. This rebellion shows up in various forms, such as pride, unbelief, and worshipping created things rather than the Creator.

Sin also distorts our relationships with one another. It leads to envy, strife, hatred, and injustice, breaking the bonds of love and trust. Our selfishness and greed result in exploitation, oppression, and a lack of compassion for our fellow human beings. This relational brokenness reflects our fractured relationship with God.

Guilt and shame are the internal consequences of sin. They are the heart's recognition of wrongdoing and the loss of innocence. These experiences indicate our awareness of violating God's standards. Likewise, suffering is a pervasive reality in a fallen world. It encompasses physical pain, emotional distress, and existential anguish. While suffering is often a direct consequence of sin, it also serves to remind us of our need for God and the hope of ultimate redemption and restoration through Jesus.

God responds to sin with both justice and mercy. He is holy and cannot tolerate sin, yet he is also loving and provides a way for redemption. Understanding the fall and sin helps us grasp the depth of human brokenness and the magnitude of God's redemptive work. Jesus is the way out of the fall and its terrible consequences. By the power of the Holy Spirit, Jesus calls us to repentance, faith, and a life transformed by God's grace.

QUESTION 16

What Has Gone Wrong?

ANSWER

The deepest source of misery in the world is not ignorance, injustice, or the failure to be true to ourselves. It is sin: cosmic treason against our Creator and his rule. Sin corrupts creation, wrecks relationships, and enslaves us to the Evil One.

SOMETHING IS AMISS IN THE WORLD. Many who grapple with the big questions of life share this uneasiness. In the face of suffering, injustice, and uncertainty, we struggle to understand what has gone wrong. *That* something is wrong is widely accepted. Just *what* is wrong and why—that's where opinions diverge.

There are many theories about what has gone wrong. Some believe the most significant source of misery lies in a lack of human knowledge. Ignorance is the culprit, and education is the solution. To combat whatever is wrong in the world, we must educate people on what is right, thus rehabilitating the mind and heart to make better choices.

Others believe the root cause of the world's problems can be traced to large-scale injustice and oppression, such as economic inequality, racism, and environmental degradation. They look to the structures of power and the institutions that govern society as the primary perpetrators of wrongdoing in the world.

More than a few believe the world's problems is rooted in obstacles that get in the way of people finding and being true to themselves. They think the solution is changing individual behavior and attitudes by appealing to whatever they feel deep inside, or whatever self-help practices will help them become the best version of themselves.

If you think the source of the world's problems is ignorance, injustice, or the failure to self-actualize, you'll think the solution is education, social activism, or self-help transformation. The Christian understanding of what's gone wrong doesn't deny every aspect of these approaches, but it goes much deeper. The problem is more than institutional injustice, lack of education, or personal failure. The most profound source of misery in the world is human sin—our rebellion against God and his rule. The consequences of that rebellion spread beyond individual suffering, leading to the world's brokenness and corruption.

To put it another way, the source of our problem is not merely horizontal—against one another; our problem is primarily vertical—we have sinned against *God.* The world's understanding of sin and suffering focuses on the horizontal perspective, seen in individual experiences or institutional failures. What's missed is the deeper, vertical reality of our relationship with God. The Bible presents sin as cosmic treason against our Creator and his rule. The fallout from that disastrous rebellion is what is wrong with the world.

Sin's consequences are many. It corrupts the whole creation, shatters relationships, and enslaves us to the Evil One. The biblical account of creation and what is often called "the fall" in the first three chapters of Genesis tells this story. God created everything and declared it good, but sin entered the world through human disobedience and rebellion against God's rule. Sin brought about brokenness, pain, and suffering in every aspect of life, including our relationships with God, others, ourselves, and the world. Sin separates us from the source of life and brings about death.

The vertical problem requires a vertical solution, and the rescue God launches is what becomes the plotline for the rest of the Bible. From Genesis to Revelation, the Bible is the story of God's overcoming love conquering our sin, Satan, and the world.

REFLECTION QUESTIONS

1. **Are you more likely to think of sin in horizontal terms or in vertical terms? Why is it important to see all sin as ultimately against God?** Reflect on the Bible's diagnosis for what's gone wrong with the world, and why so many of the world's explanations for the world's brokenness don't go deep enough.

2. **What are the effects of your sin on those closest to you?** Contemplate the fallout for when you've sinned in the past. How have your relationships been affected? How have you sought to make things right with others?

3. **Why is it important that we trace the problems in this world back to their root cause (sin)?** Think about all that goes wrong in the world. Consider how we might maintain a Godward-oriented understanding of sin that leads to all the problems we face in society.

SCRIPTURE REFERENCES

- Genesis 3:1-19
- Isaiah 59:2
- Jeremiah 17:9
- John 8:34
- Romans 3:23-24
  Romans 6:23
  Romans 8:18-25
- Ephesians 2:1-10
- James 1:13-15
- 1 John 1:8-10
  1 John 3:4

QUESTION 17

What Form Does Our Sin Take Against God?

ANSWER

We love God's gifts more than we love the Giver of all good things. We push God from the center and place our trust in ourselves and other created things—dishonoring his name, defying his Word, and disbelieving his love.

FOR MANY PEOPLE TODAY, ANY notion of sin is merely a social construct created by religious institutions to maintain power and control over their followers. Sin isn't real; it's a religious invention with little relevance to modern society. The old-fashioned concept of sin implies there is a divine authority we must obey. It is judgmental and divisive, promoting guilt and shame rather than compassion and understanding. If sin *does* exist, it is a personal issue; it has nothing to do with a higher moral standard. It's just the failure to live up to our ideals and values.

In contrast to this understanding of sin, the Bible lays out an unmistakable vertical dimension that emphasizes the form our sin takes against God. Even churchgoers might think of sin as simply making mistakes or might think of themselves as merely the victims of suffering and evil, never the perpetrators. But the sin that wreaks havoc in our world is not a minor infraction; it's high treason. It is idolatry—the act of loving God's gifts more than God the Giver. It is exchanging the glory of the immortal God for created things, for something else we believe might satisfy the longing in our souls.

If it's true that God is the center and point of everything, sin is the attempt to push him from the center—to trust ourselves or look for happiness in something created rather than the Creator. That's why, in the Bible, sin is never just a private matter but a public offense. We dishonor the name of God. We defy his Word. Instead of trusting in him, we trust ourselves. We disbelieve his love, which strikes at the heart of our identity as beloved persons made in God's image.

The Bible describes sin as something far greater than a temporary lapse; it's a chronic disease. Our sin against God is not a one-time mistake or occasional slip but a pervasive and chronic condition that affects every aspect of our being. It manifests itself in our thoughts, desires, and actions, and leads to brokenness and dysfunction in our relationships with God, others, and ourselves.

When we consider the form our sin takes against God, we see a cosmic tragedy unfolding that has marred the beauty and harmony of God's creation. It has brought suffering, pain, and death into the world and has separated us from God and one another. As the apostle Paul writes, "All have sinned and fall short of the glory of God" (Romans 3:23). Make no mistake. Sin is ugly. And until we get a grip on just how ugly sin is, we will never fully comprehend the gospel story. We will never appreciate all we have been saved *to* until we first understand what we have been saved *from*.

REFLECTION QUESTIONS

1. **Consider the three ways our sin is directed toward God (dishonoring his name, defying his Word, and disbelieving his love). Which of these three most resonates with you?** What are some of the most common sinful attitudes and actions directed toward God in our time?

2. **What are some signs that you are attempting to push God from the center and trust in yourself?** Consider specific instances where you have prioritized your desires over God's will. How have your choices affected your relationships with others and your overall spiritual wellbeing?

3. **What are the most common expressions of idolatry you wrestle with?** Think about the ways we love the gifts of God more than we love him as the Giver. What are the most common idols in our day? Why are they powerful?

SCRIPTURE REFERENCES

- Genesis 3:1-24
- Exodus 20:1-17
- Deuteronomy 8:19
- Psalm 51:1-19
  Psalm 106:19-21
- Isaiah 42:8
  Isaiah 53:1-12
- Jeremiah 2:13
- Matthew 6:24
- Romans 1:25
  Romans 3:9-26
  Romans 8:7
- Ephesians 2:1-10
- James 4:4
- 1 John 1:5-10

QUESTION 18

What Form Does Our Sin Take Against One Another?

ANSWER

We use each other, treating people like things, and things like people. We love ourselves more than our neighbors, diminishing them through dishonor and injury, lust and exploitation, falsehood and envy.

LISTEN TO POP MUSIC TODAY from just about any famous artist and you'll hear songs about relational conflict and personal hurt. Artists give voice to their lament and anger in a world of hatred, jealousy, and betrayal. Look at social media and you'll see public feuds, shaming tactics, and vicious trolling. Listen to people talk and you'll hear them describe others as "toxic" or "narcissistic" or "harmful."

Why do relationships break down? Why do we hurt each other so much? Some attribute relational conflict to racism, economic disparity, or social injustice. Others blame political polarization or religious intolerance. Many see their relational challenges as flowing directly from past trauma or present insecurity. While all these factors may play a role in relational breakdown in society, the Bible takes a step further, pointing us to the deeper issue of sin. Our rebellion against God is the root cause of our broken relationships. And sin disrupts not only our relationship with God but also with each other. Radically, the Bible teaches the problem isn't *out there* in the world but *in our own hearts*.

According to the Scriptures, we were created to love God and love each other, but sin has distorted this design, turning our love inward. We are turned in on ourselves. We give in to a selfish impulse that leads us to act in ways contrary to God's will. Our selfishness affects us and those around us. Instead of honoring and serving others, we seek to exploit them and use them for our gain.

Six of the Ten Commandments (see the Appendix for the full list) focus on the horizontal effects of our sin: our failure to honor our father and mother, murder, adultery, theft, bearing false witness, and coveting what someone else has. Relational brokenness shows up in these various ways: dishonor, injury, lust, exploitation, falsehood, and envy.

The world's solutions to relational breakdown do not come with the wisdom or resources God provides. They aren't comprehensive enough. The cause of our relational problems can't be reduced to societal factors or personal differences; the reasons for relational strife indicate a deeper spiritual condition.

Scripture helps us see how our sin against others takes place both through external actions and internal attitudes. Sin is not just about what we do but also the state of our hearts. Adultery stems from lust. Murder from anger. Theft from envy.

Our sin against one another reflects our broken relationship with God. When we push God out of the center, we naturally place ourselves and our desires above others. This self-centeredness leads us to use people for our purposes, treating them as a means to an end rather than as valuable individuals made in God's image. We treat people like things (diminishing and reducing them as persons), and we treat things like people (lifting up idols, our careers, our possessions).

This is what it looks like when our sin is directed toward other people. The Bible's diagnosis is stark, explaining the reason we suffer the effects of others who sin against us, while also exposing the ways others have suffered when we've sinned against them.

REFLECTION QUESTIONS

1. **What are some contemporary examples of the sins listed above (dishonor, lust, exploitation, injury, etc.)?** Reflect on different attitudes and actions that display these ways of sinning against other people.

2. **What has been your experience in feeling the effects of other people's sins against you? How have you responded when you've realized you have sinned against others?** Consider specific moments when you have caused harm to others. How can you seek forgiveness and reconciliation in these relationships, and what steps can you take to prevent such actions in the future?

3. **How does Christianity's diagnosis of sin help us better understand the root causes of relational conflict?** How can you pursue forgiveness, reconciliation, and restoration in your interactions with those around you?

SCRIPTURE REFERENCES

- Exodus 20:1-17
- Matthew 5:21-24
  Matthew 18:21-22
  Matthew 22:37-39
- Romans 3:23
  Romans 13:9
- Galatians 5:19-21
- Ephesians 4:31-32
- Philippians 2:3-4
- Colossians 3:5-9
- James 3:14-16
  James 4:1-2
- 1 Peter 2:1
- 1 John 3:17

QUESTION 19
How Does God Respond to Sin?

ANSWER

God is not a permissive grandfather who winks at sin, but a perfect Father of fiery love. He hates sin because it defies his righteous character, disrupts our fellowship with him, and defaces us—his beloved image-bearers.

"IT'S MY JOB TO SIN; it's God's job to forgive me." So goes the thinking in a world where sin, if there is such a thing, is a personal failure to live up to one's own ideals and standards, not an offense against a holy God. Even among those who believe in a higher power, the idea of God as wrathful toward sin is distasteful, something the psychologist Carl Jung described as a projection of unconscious fears and insecurities. Some thinkers, such as Ayn Rand, remade selfishness into a virtue rather than a vice. What's truly immoral, she'd say, is to act against your self-interest or to sacrifice for others. Others admit our selfish impulses must be resisted, but as part of our own personal and psychological betterment, not because we've offended God or failed to love our neighbors as ourselves.

The Bible paints a different picture of the seriousness of sin and selfishness. In Scripture, we don't see God winking at sin as if he were a permissive grandfather. We don't see him sweeping the effects of sin under the rug or shrugging his shoulders at evil in the world. His response is not sentimental. He doesn't minimize sin's causes and effects. Instead, we see God thundering against sin, expressing his hatred of evil. He responds to sin as a direct affront to his glory and righteousness.

Why does the Bible insist on this response from God to sin? The answer may surprise you. God's hatred of sin is rooted in his holy love. It is because God is love that God hates sin. If sin separates us from God and severs us from the source of all life (thus leading to spiritual death), how could God be loving if he remained indifferent to our plight?

God stands implacably opposed to sin because of his great love for his glory and the good of those he made in his image. Sin defies his righteous character. Sin disrupts our fellowship with him. Even more, sin defaces us, leading to our destruction. If God were to stand at a distance, shrugging at the defacement of the beloved persons he made in his image, passive in the face of evil destroying his good creation, we would question his love for all he has made.

God hates sin because it represents a betrayal of his love and goodness. Sin strikes at his glory and righteousness. He also hates sin because of what it does to us, how it alters and disfigures us. The palatable, softened vision of God so often on display in our world today doesn't fit the picture we see in the Bible—a God of fiery love, a blazing sun of holiness and mercy, whose white-hot wrath toward sin stems from the volcano of his undying, everlasting love for his people.

REFLECTION QUESTIONS

1. **What are some signs that we don't take sin as seriously as God does?** Reflect on whether you minimize, justify, or take sin seriously. How does your view of sin impact your relationship with God and others?

2. **What is the biggest obstacle to understanding God's view of sin in our society?** Consider the cultural perspectives that might hinder a proper understanding of sin as an offense against God. How can you address these obstacles in your own life and conversations with others?

3. **Why is it important to see God's hatred of sin as rooted in his love?** What happens when we fail to connect God's anger toward sin to his love for people? What about when we minimize God's anger and sentimentalize his response to sin?

SCRIPTURE REFERENCES

- Psalm 5:4-5
  Psalm 51:17
- Proverbs 15:9
- Isaiah 59:2
  Isaiah 64:6-7
- Jeremiah 17:9-10
- Habakkuk 1:13
- Romans 1:18
  Romans 3:23-24
  Romans 6:23
- 2 Corinthians 5:17-19
- James 4:8-10
- 1 John 1:8-9

QUESTION 20

Why Do We Feel Guilt and Shame?

ANSWER

Guilt tells us we have violated God's Word. Shame tells us to hide from God and from each other. Deliverance comes not through our power to resist guilt and shame but through God's provision to remove their source—our sin.

FOR MANY TODAY, FEELINGS of guilt and shame are nothing more than a warped social construct, a product of oppressive religious systems seeking to control and manipulate individuals. The solution is to liberate ourselves from these feelings and embrace our true selves without judgment or condemnation, to pursue a path of self-acceptance and self-affirmation, detached from any moral standards or objective truth. Unfortunately, this solution is like treating a symptom rather than a disease. We can't shake all our feelings of guilt and shame, no matter how hard we try.

The Bible explains the cause of guilt and shame and explains why we're so often unable to rid ourselves of these feelings. When we lean *into* these feelings to see where they lead, we find them to be signposts pointing us toward the hope of forgiveness and healing. Guilt and shame persist because they are grounded in *fact,* not just feeling. They stem from our broken relationship with God. In the garden of Eden, when the man and woman disobeyed God's command, they experienced guilt and shame. They violated God's Word and were guilty before him. Then they covered themselves and hid from God in shame.

In the Bible, guilt is the result of disobeying God's moral law and failing to live up to his righteous standards. It underscores the reality that we have sinned against a holy and just God and deserve his righteous judgment. Guilt clues us into our need for forgiveness and reconciliation with God. Shame results from our awareness of our fallen state. It underscores our vulnerability, the defacing of the image of God in us. Shame points us to our need for restoration and healing, acknowledging that we need someone to restore the cracked image and renew us inside and out.

We all experience guilt and shame because we live in a fallen world marred by sin and brokenness. Sometimes we may experience false feelings of guilt and shame. This too is part of life in a fallen world, when our feelings get distorted, and we labor under lies. Christianity offers the solution for both true and false feelings of guilt and shame: a path to redemption through the sacrificial love of Jesus.

In a world that sees guilt and shame as burdens to avoid at all costs, Christianity teaches that a proper understanding of guilt and shame can catalyze personal growth and transformation. It can reveal our deep-seated need for acceptance, worth, and belonging. We are invited to embrace our identity as beloved children of God, finding healing and wholeness in the arms of our loving Creator.

Guilt reveals our transgressions against God's perfect standard, while shame compels us to conceal our brokenness. True freedom from guilt and shame is found in God's provision to remove the source of our sin and restore us to a right relationship with him.

REFLECTION QUESTIONS

1. **In what ways do guilt and shame show up in your life?** Reflect on how these feelings affect your thoughts, emotions, and relationships. How might you bring these burdens before God for healing and forgiveness?

2. **What are the ways people try to cope with feelings of guilt and shame?** Consider whether these coping mechanisms are helpful or detrimental to finding true healing and restoration. How can

you seek God's grace and the support of a Christian community in dealing with guilt and shame?

3. **Why is it important to remember the objective standard of God's holiness when considering our guilt and shame?** Reflect on the difference between the world's vision of guilt and shame as merely subjective feelings and the Bible's portrayal of guilt and shame as rooted in the reality of sin. How does this difference affect our understanding of sin and salvation?

SCRIPTURE REFERENCES

- Genesis 3:10
- Psalm 32:5
  Psalm 51:3-4
- Isaiah 61:7
- Romans 3:23
  Romans 7:24-25
- 2 Corinthians 7:10
- Hebrews 10:22
- 1 John 1:9

QUESTION 21
What Is Suffering?

ANSWER

Suffering is the experience of physical, emotional, or spiritual pain—a mark of life in a fallen world. Suffering is real and mysterious, but never meaningless, because God makes use of suffering to shape our character and increase our faith.

"AN ESSENTIAL PART OF THE teachings and directives of the great religious and philosophical thinkers the world over has been the meaning of pain and suffering,"[1] wrote the German philosopher Max Scheler. Every society lives by spoken or unspoken teachings and traditions that help make sense of the world. Essential to any overarching world story is the meaning of suffering and how best to respond to it.

In today's world, we often encounter four different understandings and responses to suffering. Some say suffering results from human choices and failures and can be eliminated through human effort and resources. This view emphasizes self-reliance. Others see life as a product of chance; suffering is just an unfortunate aspect of life on earth, carrying no real significance. Some religions see suffering as an illusion caused by attachment to the material world, which can be transcended through the destruction of desire. Finally, many point to suffering due to societal or systemic failures, prioritizing the need for social and political change.

While there is truth to be found in these views, Christianity doesn't line up completely with any of them. The Bible teaches that suffering is real and unavoidable, its causes and effects often mysterious, and yet suffering is never meaningless. The Old Testament book of Job is an exploration of suffering, never giving easy answers or simplistic solutions, and it stands as one of the greatest literary works of all time. God has promised to make use of suffering, and one day to eliminate all sorrow forever.

In Romans 5:3-4, the apostle Paul writes: "We also glory in our sufferings, because we know that suffering produces perseverance; perseverance, character; and character, hope" (NIV). Seen in this light, suffering is not meaningless but can be used by God to develop and shape our character. This does not mean that suffering is enjoyable or easily explainable; it simply means God can and will use it to produce spiritual growth and maturity.

How should we respond to suffering? With gentleness and patience. Sometimes, suffering results from sins we have committed or the sins someone has committed against us. Other times, suffering is part of living in a broken world. It is wrong to assume that a vibrant faith or dedicated obedience to God will preserve us from the experience of suffering.

Many find suffering to be a stumbling block for believing in God, and understandably so. But even if the Bible does not give us a fully exhaustive account of why God permits so much suffering in this world, the gospel story demonstrates that God is not indifferent to our pain. If it's true that the Son of God willingly entered the worst of human suffering, then, in Christ, God knows what it means to suffer. He is *with* us in our sorrow.

Isaiah 42 describes the mysterious Suffering Servant who, Isaiah 53 reveals, will have the guilt of our transgressions put upon him so that, by his suffering, our condemnation will be taken away. This is the great hope spread over the pages of the Bible—God knows how to care for the fragile. He loves to care for the bruised and battered. He is the one who enters our suffering, promises to bind up our broken hearts and heal our wounds (Psalm 147:3; Isaiah 61:1).

REFLECTION QUESTIONS

1. **How have you coped with the experience of suffering in the past?** Reflect on your reactions when faced with suffering. How does your response align with the understanding that suffering can shape your character and increase your faith?

2. **How does your understanding of suffering shape how you view God and his character?** Consider how your experiences with

suffering influence your perception of God's nature. How can you reconcile the reality of suffering with believing in a loving and merciful God who promises our suffering is never meaningless?

3. **How can you be more mindful and compassionate toward others experiencing suffering?** Think about ways you can support and empathize with those who are suffering. How can you offer your presence as a comfort? Why should Christians be involved in alleviating suffering in a fallen world?

SCRIPTURE REFERENCES

- Psalm 34:18
- Isaiah 53:3-5
- Romans 5:3-5
- 2 Corinthians 1:3-4
2 Corinthians 4:17-18
- Philippians 3:10-11
- 2 Timothy 2:12
- Hebrews 12:11
- James 1:2-4
- 1 Peter 1:2-4, 6-7

PART 4

Story of Redemption

The story of redemption is the grand narrative of God's rescue plan to restore humanity and creation from the devastation of sin. This plan is revealed through the history of Israel and culminates in Jesus Christ's life, death, resurrection, and ascension.

God's rescue plan begins with Abraham's call and the formation of Israel, a people chosen to reflect God's holiness and love for the nations. Through Israel's sacrificial system, we learn about the gravity of sin and the necessity of atonement. The history of Israel's kings teaches us the need for a righteous ruler who can lead with justice and mercy. The prophets of Israel further reveal God's heart and his promises, calling the people to repentance and foretelling the coming of the Messiah.

Jesus of Nazareth fulfills all these hopes and prophecies. He is God incarnate, who lived a sinless life, taught with divine authority, and demonstrated the kingdom of God through miracles and acts of compassion. On the cross, Jesus took upon himself the punishment for our sins, providing the way for reconciliation with God. Jesus's resurrection is the cornerstone of the Christian faith, confirming his victory over sin and death, offering us the hope of eternal life. His ascension emphasizes his exalted position at the Father's right hand, where he intercedes for us and rules over all creation.

Pentecost marks the outpouring of the Holy Spirit upon believers, empowering them to continue Jesus's mission on earth. The Spirit's presence inaugurates the new covenant and equips the church to bear witness to the gospel, transforming lives and advancing God's kingdom.

QUESTION 22

How Does God's Rescue Plan Unfold?

ANSWER

God called Abraham and promised to create a worldwide family of faith. He rescued the children of Israel, gave them the Law, and called them to be a light to the nations. Salvation comes not through human ingenuity but divine initiative.

EVERYWHERE YOU TURN, YOU FIND gurus who say the starting point for personal success, fulfillment, and salvation is in yourself. *The world is what you make it... Your decisions determine your destiny... You have the power to create your destiny, shape your reality, and make meaning on your terms.* Ultimate authority and absolute agency are in your hands. Through the ingenuity of human thought and action, we can fix what's wrong with the world, and with ourselves.

The Bible has a different starting point. We don't begin with a self-help plan engineered by people, but with a rescue plan initiated by God. God moves first in salvation. Grace comes first. In Genesis 12, we see this rescue plan go into motion, when God called an ordinary man, Abraham, and promised to bless him and make his descendants a great nation through which blessing would flow to the world.

God's choice of Abraham rubs many people the wrong way. Why choose just one person? Why work through one nation? Why can't there be multiple paths to salvation? Isn't it unfair that God implements his plan through a particular people? These questions arise because they come into conflict with the assumption that all paths lead to God, or that all religious expressions are equally valid, or that salvation is something we deserve.

But just as the Bible demotes us in making God to be the center and point of everything, so also God's rescue plan demotes us in making clear it is God's power and purpose that prevails, not our own. Once we understand God's rescue plan from a biblical perspective, we find liberation from the burden of attempting to achieve salvation on our own. We experience peace and assurance when we respond to God's grace that goes before us and marks out the way.

As the Old Testament story unfolds, we meet the patriarchs: Abraham, Isaac, and Jacob (Israel). We hear the groaning of the Israelites in slavery to Egypt, and watch God raise up a deliverer, Moses, to lead them out of captivity and into the promised land. God gives his people the Ten Commandments as part of the Law intended to guide them in righteousness. The Law is a gift that reveals the holiness of God. By obeying the Law, God's people are to be a light to the nations, showing the rest of the world the breadth and depth of God's heart for humanity.

The call of Abraham reminds us that our lives are part of an ongoing saga, each of us intricately woven into God's redemptive plan, pointing us to the ultimate fulfillment that can only be found in his salvation. Once we believe the Bible's description of this divine rescue plan, we can reject our paltry attempts to achieve salvation for ourselves, recognize the beauty of God's divine initiative, and rest in his providential plan to bring about redemption for his glory and our good.

REFLECTION QUESTIONS

1. **How does the Bible's vision of salvation as God's initiative stand in contrast to the prevailing notion that we determine our destiny and achieve fulfillment on our own?** Reflect on how modern values of individualism and self-sufficiency shape your perception of fulfillment and destiny. How do these values align or conflict with the Christian belief in God's unfolding plan and divine initiative?

2. **In what ways have you experienced the tension between trying to fix the world (or yourself) on your own and the biblical teaching that God's rescue plan requires surrender and trust?** Consider moments when you felt the pull between following your path and

trusting God's plan. How have these experiences affected your faith and understanding of God's purpose for your life?

3. **Reflect on the story of Abraham and his call from God. What can we learn from his journey of faith and the promises God made to him?** Consider Abraham's journey and its reliance on God's promises and timing. How can his story inspire and guide your faith journey, especially in uncertain or waiting times?

SCRIPTURE REFERENCES

- Genesis 12:1-3
- Exodus 6:6-7
  Exodus 19:5-6
- Deuteronomy 7:6-8
- Psalm 67:1-2
- Isaiah 42:6-7
  Isaiah 49:6
- John 14:6
- Acts 4:12
  Acts 10:34-35
  Acts 13:47
- Romans 9:6-8
- Galatians 3:8-9
- 1 Peter 2:9-10

QUESTION 23

What Do We Learn from Israel's Sacrificial System?

ANSWER

No earthly system of sacrifice can fully atone for sin. We cannot get right with God by willpower or good works. We need a perfect mediator to represent us to God and represent God to us.

"**BELIEVE THOROUGHLY IN YOUR GREATER** interior self. Know that you have something within you that is greater than any obstacle, circumstance or difficulty you can possibly meet."[1] So said Christian Larson in a book from 1910, *Your Forces and How to Use Them.* Nearly a century later, Oprah Winfrey, at a commencement speech for Stanford University said something similar: "The greatest discovery of all time is that a person can change his future by merely changing his attitude."[2]

It's common sense today that the way to get right with God is to get right with ourselves. With the right attitude, persistence in good deeds, and a commitment to self-improvement, we can move past our failures and flaws to find absolution and fulfillment. We need to forgive ourselves for our sins, so we can be free from feelings of inadequacy and inferiority.

The Bible presents something different: a radically God-centered view of what's wrong with us. Because our sin is ultimately directed upward (against God), the solution must come from above, not from within. And nowhere is the serious nature of sin more clearly shown in the Old Testament than the lengthy and detailed instructions about the temple and the sacrificial system we find in the book of Leviticus.

Leviticus reveals the severity of our sin problem. Through the instructions given in the Law, we see God's temporary provision for bringing his people back into fellowship with him through offerings and sacrifices overseen by priests. We see pictures of cleansing and healing, so we can once again be clean and whole. We see pictures of substitution, where an innocent, spotless lamb is sacrificed in place of the guilty person in need of atonement. We see pictures of gratitude for God's provision and blessing, however undeserved. We see sin being sent away, removed forever from the presence of God. We see pictures of restoration, so the sinner can once again join the community of faith freely.

With its rules and regulations, Leviticus may seem distant and irrelevant to modern readers, but its central themes of atonement and sanctity set the course for the rest of the Bible. Sin contaminates everything. Leviticus even has a category for unknown sins (Leviticus 5:17).

The Law shows us God's holiness and the chasm sin creates between us and God. We are far more sinful than we even know. But the Law also points forward to the grace of God that is greater than we could imagine. By providing a sacrificial system, and by giving us the initial outline of a painting whose brush strokes would later be filled in by the sacrifice of Jesus, God reveals his heart—he wants to be with his people, to forgive our sins and cleanse us of unrighteousness. Understanding the gravity of our sin, God's holiness, and the price of atonement helps us appreciate our need for a Great High Priest, who will not only fulfill the old system of atonement, but also give us a preview of what is to come—a renewed world where we live in perfect communion with God, forever free from sin's stains.

REFLECTION QUESTIONS

1. **What are some ways our society tends to diminish or minimize the severity of sin?** Reflect on cultural understandings of sin and how they align with or differ from what the Bible says.

2. **What do we learn from the detailed instructions we find in the Law regarding the sacrificial system?** Reflect on these pictures

of our sin and our need for atonement. How do these pictures challenge contemporary views of moving past our sins, of forgiving ourselves, or making things right on our own?

3. **How does the reality of God's provision of atonement affect our day-to-day thoughts and actions as we live the Christian life?** What practices would show gratitude for Jesus's intercession and sacrifice? How can we better rest in God's provision for salvation instead of living as if we must atone for our sins ourselves?

SCRIPTURE REFERENCES

- Exodus 3:12
  Exodus 19:5-6
- Leviticus 16:30
  Leviticus 17:11
- Psalm 51:16-17
- Isaiah 53:4-6
- Matthew 5:17
- John 1:14, 29
- Romans 3:23-24
  Romans 6:22
  Romans 8:34
- 2 Corinthians 5:21
- Galatians 2:16
- Hebrews 4:14
  Hebrews 7:25
  Hebrews 10:1-4, 12-14
- 1 Timothy 2:5-6
- Revelation 21:3-4

QUESTION 24
What Do We Learn from Israel's Kings?

ANSWER

No sinner can fulfill God's intent for humanity to rule with perfect wisdom and righteousness over creation. Even the best kings of Israel failed this high calling. We need a perfect King to provide eternal protection and peace.

EVERY ELECTION CYCLE, PEOPLE PLACE their hopes on a preferred candidate who promises to usher in a better future. Factions arise, coalitions form, and tribal impulses dominate. As the years go by, people are inevitably disappointed. Even the best attempts at achieving justice and peace go wrong in one way or another. History is full of tyrants and dictators who sought to impose their will and make the world a better place through force. And despite the horror of past tyrannies, the desire for a ruler to establish a new order, to make everything right even if it requires violence, continues to surface in many societies.

The pendulum swings from good rulers to tyrants, from political hope to disappointment. None of this comes as a surprise if we immerse ourselves in the unfolding story we find in the Bible. In the Scriptures, we see the tendency for rulers and authorities to go bad, but we also recognize why there's a deep longing in the human heart for a king to make things right. We desire autonomy and self-rule, yet paradoxically, we often pin our hopes and expectations on flawed and fallible political leaders. Paradoxically, we reject the idea of a king, yet we still long for a savior and look for groups of people or various schemes to deliver what we desire deep down.

As the scene shifts from the rescued Israelites receiving the Law (Exodus) to their entrance into the promised land (Joshua), we see a succession of kings, some who followed the Lord and brought peace and justice for the people and others who were half-hearted or who rebelled against God in how they ruled. First came Saul, David, and Solomon. Then the kingdom split into a Northern Kingdom (Israel) and a Southern Kingdom (Judah), and many more kings followed.

One of the striking features of the Bible is its honesty about the failures of even the best of Israel's kings. The heroes of the Bible, such as David and Solomon, are not enshrined in rose-colored stained-glass windows. We see their virtues and their vices, their sanctity and their sins. And through their stories, we learn that no earthly king or political system can bring true and lasting fulfillment.

Why do we still long for a king? Because God originally intended human beings to rule wisely over his creation, subdue the earth, and exercise generous authority. Due to sin, history reveals a line of flawed and failing attempts to fulfill this vocation through various political visions. No wonder that for some, the idea of authority is itself oppressive. Unfortunately, every attempt at implementing a perfect democracy has ended in anarchy or tyranny.

Recognizing human rulers' limitations and failures, we face the reality that no sinner can fulfill God's original intent for humanity to rule with total wisdom and righteousness. Even the best kings of Israel fell short of this high calling, reminding us of our need for a perfect King to come.

REFLECTION QUESTIONS

1. **In what ways have you experienced the limitations and failures of human leaders and systems in your own life?** Reflect on personal experiences with political leaders, societal systems, or authority figures. How did these experiences shape your views on human governance and the need for a perfect, divine ruler?

2. **Reflect on the significance of Israel's kings and the Bible's honest portrayal of both their greatness and their sin.** How do the stories of the Old Testament break us of utopian fantasies or help us approach today's political realm with realism?

3. **In what ways is the human longing for a king to make things right visible in our world? In what ways is resistance to kingship and authority also visible?** Consider the paradox of why we both long for and resist the idea of a king ruling over us. How does the Bible help us understand these seemingly contradictory impulses?

SCRIPTURE REFERENCES

- 1 Samuel 8:6-7
- 1 Kings 15:11
- Psalm 2:10-12
  Psalm 146:3-4
- Isaiah 55:8-9
- Jeremiah 17:5-8
  Jeremiah 23:5-6
- Ezekiel 37:24-25
- Matthew 21:5
- John 18:36-37
- Hebrews 4:14-16
- Revelation 19:16

QUESTION 25

What Do We Learn from Israel's Prophets?

ANSWER

No human philosophy can fully enlighten the mind or cure the heart. The prophets to Israel delivered God's message and pointed ahead to a divine prophet who would not only explain, but embody his Word.

IT'S COMMON TODAY FOR PEOPLE to assume that morality and truth is determined by the individual. We don't need prophets or religious figures to tell us what is right or wrong. Every person is responsible for creating their own moral compass. Therefore, the idea of divine revelation or a prophet who speaks on behalf of God is a relic of the past.

According to this outlook, truth is subjective and personal, enlightenment is self-driven, and the idea of a prophet as a divine messenger from God seems silly. That said, this outlook doesn't stop us from frequently looking to modern prophets for wisdom and guidance. They're creating podcasts, hosting channels online, or launching tirades on social media. Instead of offering a fresh perspective or divine insight, modern prophets usually cater to their audience's desires and preferences. They may claim to have something unique to say, but their message is often just a remix of whatever trends are most popular. They affirm and validate popular ideologies and rarely provide a sharp edge or challenge.

The prophets we see in the Bible are different. Yes, there were some false prophets who merely echoed whatever the prevailing powers wanted to hear. But the true prophets stood out. These prophets were not mere human philosophers or moral guides. God chose them to deliver his message of divine truth to his people. They spoke with authority, not based on personal opinions or cultural trends, but on behalf of God himself.

The Old Testament prophets were known for *foretelling* and *forth-telling*. Foretelling refers to the prophet's ability to predict future events, while forth-telling refers to proclaiming the truth of God's Word in the present moment. Both aspects are essential in understanding the ministry of prophets.

The Bible gives us numerous examples of prophets who foretold events with remarkable accuracy. They spoke from God about the coming judgment, the rise and fall of nations, the exile of God's people, and the end of the exile through the promised Messiah. But the role of the prophet was not limited to predicting the future. They also played the vital function of delivering the truth of God's Word for the present moment. They confronted the people with their sins, called for repentance, and urged them to return to God. The prophets spoke against injustice, idolatry, and hypocrisy. They challenged people to live according to God's commandments and to pursue righteousness.

The Bible is clear on our need for revelation, a divine voice that pierces through the noise of would-be prophets and gurus who all paint their own pictures of what the good life looks like. We need more than the echo of our times; we need the authoritative voice of God to guide us and lead us to the fullness of his purposes. We need more than human enlightenment; we need the light of God's divine revelation to illuminate our path. The Old Testament prophets pointed forward to the divine prophet, Jesus the Messiah, who would not only explain but also embody the Word of God.

REFLECTION QUESTIONS

1. **What are the go-to sources for enlightenment and self-betterment in our world today?** Reflect on influencers and thought leaders and their messages of personal growth and fulfillment. How do the biblical prophets speaking on behalf of God align with or counter some of these messages?

2. **Consider the significance of the prophetic ministry's foretelling and forth-telling aspects.** Which aspect stands out more to you? How do both aspects help us see the heart of God?

3. **What cultural trends or narratives today are most clearly countered by the Old Testament prophets?** Consider the sins they called out, and the comfort they brought to anyone willing to turn from sin and turn back to God. Identify areas in your daily interactions and conversations where you can serve as a prophetic voice, standing firm in God's truth.

SCRIPTURE REFERENCES

- Isaiah 6:8-9
  Isaiah 9:6-7
- Jeremiah 1:4-10
- Ezekiel 2:3-4
- Amos 3:7
- Matthew 5:17-20
- John 1:14
- Acts 3:22-23
- 1 Corinthians 14:1-5
- Ephesians 4:11-13
- Hebrews 1:1-2

QUESTION 26

Who Is Jesus of Nazareth?

ANSWER

Jesus of Nazareth is the sinless Son of God, born of the virgin Mary. He is more than a teacher or moral guide. His words and works give us the true meaning of God's Law and a preview of God's promise to make all things new.

WHO IS JESUS? EVERYONE IN the world should wrestle with this question. Who is this man who inspires such devotion worldwide 2,000 years after he walked the earth? Who is this person whose life is the foundation for our calendar, with BC and AD revolving around his birth? Who is this man who causes so much controversy, whose followers consistently clash with the empires of this world and willingly go to their deaths rather than renounce their allegiance? Who is this Jesus?

Some take a historical perspective. Jesus was a Jewish teacher who ran afoul of the Roman authorities and got himself killed. Others think of Jesus as just a good teacher or a moral guide. He lived 2,000 years ago, gained many followers, taught people how to love God and love each other, and then was killed for his message of love to all people.

The Gospels go further, presenting Jesus as the sinless Son of God. Sinless, in that he lived the perfect life we could not live, fulfilling God's original intent for humanity and the human vocation that had been marred by sin. Son of God, seen in part through the strangeness of Jesus's birth, which came about through supernatural circumstances. His mother was a young Jewish virgin girl named Mary.

The Gospels certainly line up with contemporary portraits of Jesus as a good teacher and a moral guide, but the biblical accounts of his life go further, showing that Jesus made massive claims about his identity. What's more, the Gospels give us more than just his words; they also show us his miraculous works. Jesus promised the release to the captives, recovery of sight to the blind, and the freeing of the oppressed (Luke 4:16-21). Jesus claimed the Spirit of God himself was upon him, so that in both his words and works, he set people free.

As we've seen, for many people today, freedom is the absence of limitations or constraints. It means blasting through boundaries, not letting anyone tell you what to do, asserting yourself, and doing whatever you want the most. Jesus would call that vision of freedom just another form of slavery. The modern idea of freedom, that you can live as you please without any constraints, is slavery to yourself and the smallness of your desires. Jesus came to set people free *for* something, to live according to the purpose that God created for us.

In his teaching ministry, we see how Jesus upheld and fulfilled the Old Testament law. He dug beneath the layers of interpretation and debate over the specifics of law-keeping and went right to the heart of God in giving us the Law in the first place. He didn't relax the standards but intensified them—holding up a pristine vision of perfect righteousness while simultaneously offering grace and mercy to all who wanted to leave behind their sin. In his healings and miracles, he showed what the world is like when God is King, giving us a preview of the future restoration. In the life and ministry of Jesus, we see the long-awaited kingdom of God arriving, the climax to Israel's story.

REFLECTION QUESTIONS

1. **What is the impact of Jesus's sinless life on your understanding of salvation?** Reflect on the implications of Jesus living a perfect life on behalf of humanity. How does this alter your perspective on self-sufficiency and personal righteousness?

2. **What are some examples of Jesus giving us the true meaning of the Old Testament Law?** Consider how Jesus angered the religious leaders of his day. In what ways did Jesus reveal the heart of God in

giving his people the Law? What are some ways that extrabiblical law-keeping can obscure the heart of God?

3. **What miracles of Jesus most stand out to you?** What is the significance of these miracles? What do they tell us about God's intention for the good of the world?

SCRIPTURE REFERENCES

- Isaiah 53:5
- Matthew 1:23
  Matthew 5:17
- John 1:1-2, 14
  John 14:6
- Acts 4:12
- Philippians 2:5-8
- Colossians 2:9
- Hebrews 4:15
- 1 Peter 2:21-24

QUESTION 27
What Happened on the Cross?

ANSWER

Jesus gave himself not only as a martyr, but as the Messiah, the atoning sacrifice for our sins. His death in our place conquers evil, conveys God's love, and creates a cross-shaped people.

FOR MANY PEOPLE TODAY, the cross of Jesus symbolizes suffering and defeat, a tragic end to a noble life. The cross is an example of pain and injustice, a reminder of the world's brokenness. It's common to think of Jesus as a martyr for a righteous cause, to see him as a man who stood for what he believed to be true, even if it meant he had to die.

But several aspects of Jesus's death don't fit the martyr story. Consider Socrates, the great philosopher who, 400 years before Jesus was born, was forced to drink poison. All accounts show Socrates accepting his fate, refusing to delay the moment. One witness says that he took the cup "most easily and gently, without the least fear or change of color or feature."[1] In contrast, Jesus didn't calmly approach his death with serenity and composure. In the garden of Gethsemane, he flinched. He was in agony. He wasn't like Socrates, refusing to delay the drinking of the poison. No, Jesus cried out for God to take this cup of suffering away from him. On the cross, he screamed: "My God, my God, why have you abandoned me?" (Matthew 27:46).

According to the Bible, there was more going on in Jesus's crucifixion than just physical torture and a martyr's death. All the evil of this world was coming upon Jesus as he took the weight of human sin upon himself, as he sensed the awful judgment of God toward sin, and as he absorbed God's holy and righteous anger, to be crushed by the curse. Jesus is unlike other martyrs. He doesn't fit the category. Jesus didn't die for a cause; he died for the world.

What does the cross mean, then, if more than a story of martyrdom? The answers are inexhaustible, but we can offer a few. First, the cross is where Jesus died for us, in our place, taking on himself the punishment we deserved. Second, the cross is where evil was unmasked and conquered, where the victory over sin and death was accomplished. Third, the cross is where we see the height and depth of God's love for humanity, in that the Son was willing to suffer with us and for us to bring us back to God. Fourth, the cross marks out the formation of a new people who will display the self-giving love of God in self-sacrificial ways, a new community united by the blood of Jesus shed for our sins.

Jesus went to the cross as Israel's Messiah, bringing to a climax Israel's story of redemption. From the opening pages of Scripture, God promised to send a deliverer. Here at the cross is the fulfillment of the sacrificial system, when Jesus became the Great High Priest and the sacrifice for sin. Here at the cross is the culmination of Israel's long line of imperfect kings, when Jesus the Servant King was wounded for our transgressions and bruised for our iniquities. Here at the cross is the divine prophet all the other prophets foretold, the embodiment of God's Word, the Suffering Servant who took upon himself our iniquity. Jesus's death doesn't just give us an inspiring vision of martyrdom or a beautiful picture of sacrifice. It gives us forgiveness and victory.

REFLECTION QUESTIONS

1. **How does the truth of Jesus's death on the cross as the atoning sacrifice for our sins shape your understanding of God's love and forgiveness?** Reflect on the significance of Jesus taking on the weight of human sin and God's judgment. How does this deepen your appreciation for God's love and the forgiveness offered through Jesus?

2. **In what ways does the cross challenge your perspective on suffering and sacrifice?** Consider how Jesus's willingness to endure suffering and sacrifice for the sake of humanity contrasts with

modern views on avoiding pain and seeking personal gain. How does this shift your understanding of suffering?

3. **Reflect on the significance of Jesus's death in your own life. How does it inspire gratitude and a desire to live for him?** Think about how the cross influences your daily decisions, relationships, and actions. How does recognizing the depth of Jesus's sacrifice motivate you to respond in gratitude and commitment to living out your faith?

SCRIPTURE REFERENCES

- Isaiah 53:4-6
- John 1:29
John 19:30
- Romans 5:8
- 2 Corinthians 5:21
- Galatians 2:20
Galatians 3:13
- Ephesians 2:16
Ephesians 5:2
- Colossians 2:13-14
- Hebrews 9:28
Hebrews 10:10
- 1 Peter 2:24
- 1 John 4:10
- Revelation 1:5

QUESTION 28
What Happened on Easter?

ANSWER

Jesus rose from the grave, bodily and visibly, in triumph over sin and death to launch God's new creation. The resurrection of Jesus is not a fairy tale, but the true story of his victory.

FOR MANY TODAY, DEATH IS just a natural part of life, a final curtain call that puts to rest any notion of life beyond the material world. We are born; we die. Whatever happens in between is whatever we decide to make of life. Some scientists and anthropologists search for ways to prolong human life, or to reinvent humanity by extending our consciousness forever, so death won't have the last word. But even in these cases, the assumption is that this life is all there is.

The central claim of Christianity is that Jesus of Nazareth was raised from the dead, bodily and visibly. Nowhere does the sharp edge of Christian teaching run up more against the rocks of a secular age than here.

Why does the seemingly implausible story of a resurrected Messiah still make sense to so many people? Perhaps it's because all the great stories of our world seem to echo, however faintly, this story of Jesus's resurrection. The poison apple that puts Snow White into the slumber of death doesn't have the last word when her prince shows up on the scene. In *The Lord of the Rings*, Gandalf the Grey battles the demons into the dark pit of death only to reappear in splendor and glory as Gandalf the White. The needle prick makes Princess Aurora a sleeping beauty until a prince comes to slay the dragon and wake her up to everlasting happiness. The epic stories we return to again and again are built upon this theme of sacrificial death followed by a triumphant return.

Some philosophers believe this human desire for resurrection and restoration, the hope for life beyond the grave, is merely a wish we project onto our religious beliefs. Or they believe the idea of resurrection is a pitiful attempt to evade the finality of death, to muffle the horror of it all. But the Bible sees this desire to overcome death as rooted in something true. J.R.R. Tolkien argued that the story of Jesus dying and rising again resembles ancient myths, except that *this* myth really happened.[1] The resurrection answers the longings that all the old fairy tales point to because it is the true, historical account of Jesus's victory.

The gospel accounts confirm the unexpected resurrection of Jesus as the beginning of God's new creation. Jesus didn't merely make possible a heavenly afterlife; he was the first to go through death and out the other side, into a new and glorious bodily life that was both similar and different to what he'd been like before. The resurrection of Jesus *bodily* means that God is redeeming and restoring his creation. The physical world is not less-than or inferior to the spiritual. God is going to renew us, body and soul. The resurrection is not the happy end after Jesus's death but the beginning of God's new creation.

REFLECTION QUESTIONS

1. **How does the resurrection of Jesus challenge the narrative of death as the ultimate end, and how does it give you hope for the future?** Reflect on the implications of Jesus's victory over death. How does this reshape your understanding of life after death and give you hope and purpose in your current life?

2. **What does the resurrection say about the value and importance of the human body?** Consider ways people downplay or diminish the value of the body, sometimes thinking the spirit is all that really matters. How does the resurrection of Jesus counter this way of thinking?

3. **Reflect on the impact of Jesus's resurrection on your own identity and purpose. What is the significance of the resurrection for your spiritual journey?** Think about how the resurrection informs your sense of self and your mission in life. How does Jesus's resurrection influence your actions, decisions, and interactions with others?

SCRIPTURE REFERENCES

- Matthew 28:5-6
- Mark 16:6
- Luke 24:5-6
- John 20:19-20
- Acts 2:24
- Romans 6:4
  Romans 8:11
- 1 Corinthians 15:20-22
- Philippians 3:10-11
- 1 Peter 1:3-4
- Revelation 1:17-18
  Revelation 21:5

QUESTION 29

What Does the Ascension Tell Us About Jesus?

ANSWER

Jesus is exalted as the true King of the world, worthy of ultimate allegiance. He intercedes for us before the Father and is present with us by the Spirit.

EVERYONE WANTS TO ASCEND. Think about the metaphors we often use: climbing the ladder of success, launching into the stratosphere, being on top of the world. Through hard work, personal ambition, and the pursuit of glory, people seek to elevate themselves over others. Promoting and exalting ourselves comes naturally when we are looking to rise above the crowd.

The story of Jesus is different because his exaltation—his ascent—only took place after his *de*scent, first in becoming a servant when he took on our humanity, and then in descending to the depths of torment on the cross, and down through the valley of the shadow of death to the grave. The New Testament authors claim that after his resurrection, Jesus appeared to many witnesses for a period of 40 days, and then, after commissioning his followers, he ascended into heaven.

The great creeds of the faith summarize this part of the gospel: *He ascended into heaven and is seated at right hand of the Father.* This is another way of saying the risen Jesus is now in heaven (God's dimension), exalted as King. We don't often use the word *exalted* to describe human beings. But we do talk about people being appointed to positions of power, or being installed in a new role, or invested with authority in a company or a government. A king is crowned and enthroned. A president goes through an inauguration ceremony.

Jesus's ascension into heaven fulfills Psalm 110 and is a sign that God has marked out Jesus as the Lord of the universe. He has been *exalted* or *installed* as the world's true King. This was always God's original intention—that a human being reign over his created world. The New Testament describes Jesus as the Last Adam, the one who fulfills God's design.

What does this mean for us? Since kingship implies allegiance, we are called to pledge our loyalty to the King who has given his life for us. Instead of grappling for positions of power and authority, seeking to one-up people as we climb the ladder of success, we follow in the steps of a King whose exaltation came after taking the lowliest place. This is the King who said, "Whoever exalts himself will be humbled, and whoever humbles himself will be exalted" (Matthew 23:12).

Seated at the right hand of God, Jesus intercedes for his people. This means Jesus is praying for us. We have access to God because of Jesus's death on the cross for our sins, his resurrection from the dead, and the intercessory role he fulfills for us, as we are swept up into the goodness and glory of the God who made us.

"I am with you always," Jesus told his disciples before he ascended, "to the end of the age" (Matthew 28:20). Because of these words, we do not speak of Jesus's absence, because we still have Jesus with us by his Spirit.

REFLECTION QUESTIONS

1. **What are some ways people in our society exalt themselves over others?** How does Jesus's exaltation, which takes place after his humiliation, confront the tendency for self-exaltation?

2. **Kingship implies allegiance. In what ways do we demonstrate our belief in Jesus as King and our allegiance to his kingdom?** What are some of the characteristics of Jesus that should be present in the lives of his followers?

3. **What is the impact of Jesus's ascension on our priorities and values?** Think about how Jesus's ascension encourages us to focus on eternal realities instead of temporary achievements. How does Jesus's exaltation change our perspective?

SCRIPTURE REFERENCES

- Psalm 110:1
- Luke 24:50-51
- John 16:7
- Acts 1:9-11
- Romans 8:34
- Ephesians 1:19-23
- Philippians 2:9-11
- Colossians 2:15
  Colossians 3:1
- 1 Timothy 2:5
- Hebrews 4:14-16
  Hebrews 7:25
- 1 Peter 3:22
- Revelation 19:16

QUESTION 30

What Happened on the Day of Pentecost?

ANSWER

Jesus sent the Holy Spirit and ignited the global mission of the church. Through the Spirit's power, not our own, we spread the gospel to the nations as a people reconciled to God and to each other.

IN 1971, JOHN LENNON RELEASED "Power to the People," a song intended as a form of rebellion against oppression by the establishment. Giving power to the people is a sentiment that still resonates with people today. If only the people had power, the world would be transformed.

The Bible both affirms and subverts this notion of giving power to the people. On one side, those who argue against concentrating all power in a single individual or an elite group of people do so because they recognize the corruption of human nature. The Bible's assessment of human nature is pessimistic because we are all inclined toward sin. On the other side, if we're looking for a world of justice and righteousness, not just any power and not just any people will do. God's plan is for his people to be animated by his Spirit. The Spirit supplies the power, and the Spirit works through his people.

Fifty days after Jesus's resurrection and ten days after Jesus's ascension, on the day of Pentecost, the Holy Spirit came in power upon his people (Acts 2). The New Testament describes the Spirit's coming with fire, which makes sense because in the Old Testament, God's presence was manifested in fire. God appeared to Moses in a burning bush (Exodus 3:1-4). He led the people in the wilderness in a pillar of fire (Exodus 13:21-22). When he came to dwell in the temple, there was fire (2 Chronicles 7:1). At Pentecost, tongues of fire appeared over the heads of the believers present (Acts 2:3). Every follower of Jesus became a burning bush because God's presence was inside them.

The day of Pentecost represents the launch of God's global mission through the church, as the promise God made to Abraham to bless all the nations of the world through his descendants takes on a new shape. At Pentecost, the gospel was preached in multiple languages simultaneously in the power of the Spirit. According to strict Islamic teachings, the Qur'an cannot be translated; it can only be interpreted. Yet at the birth of the Christian church, we have the story of what happened on the day of Pentecost, when people of a score of different nations heard the mighty works of God communicated to them in their languages. The global mission on display at Pentecost means that there's not just one culture that is the right culture. The gospel can enter a culture without erasing all its distinctives, and then challenge it, lift it, change it, redeem it, and bring it into a fullness it would otherwise lack.

On the day of Pentecost, people believed in the Lord Jesus and were baptized. All this was the outworking of the Spirit poured out on the church. *Power to the people,* yes, but it's the Spirit's power poured out on Jesus's people.

As followers of Jesus, we recognize our need for the Spirit's power and presence in our lives, families, churches, and communities. The Spirit regenerates, sanctifies, gives victory over sin, teaches, unifies, and empowers our witness. The Spirit creates profound oneness in the people of God, destroys barriers, brings peace, and fills us with the power to complete the mission.

REFLECTION QUESTIONS

1. **Power is often associated with personal achievement and control in today's world. How does the outpouring of the Holy Spirit on the day of Pentecost differ from this notion of power?** Reflect on the differences between secular and spiritual power. How does the Holy Spirit's empowerment redefine your understanding of true strength and influence?

2. **The world values self-sufficiency and individual striving for power. In what ways does the outpouring of the Holy Spirit highlight the importance of dependence on God's power rather than our abilities?** Consider areas in your life where you rely on your strength. How can you shift toward a greater dependence on the Holy Spirit and recognize his work in your daily efforts and achievements?

3. **How does the multicultural and multilingual nature of the outpouring of the Holy Spirit on Pentecost challenge the world's tendency toward cultural isolation and division?** Reflect on the significance of the Holy Spirit bringing diverse people together. How can you embrace and promote unity in diversity within your community and beyond, following the example set at Pentecost?

SCRIPTURE REFERENCES

- Isaiah 40:29-31
- Joel 2:28-32
- Zechariah 4:6
- John 14:15-17
- Acts 1:8
  Acts 2:1-13
- Romans 8:9-11
  Romans 12:4-8
- 1 Corinthians 12:4-13
- Galatians 3:28
  Galatians 5:22-23
- Ephesians 3:16-19
  Ephesians 4:3-4

PART 5

Salvation by the Spirit

Salvation by the Spirit describes God's transformative work in a believer's life. This journey begins with repentance and faith. Repentance is a Spirit-enabled turning away from sin and heartfelt sorrow for offending God. It involves a change of mind and direction, where we abandon our rebellious ways and seek God's forgiveness and grace. Faith is a Spirit-given trust in Jesus Christ as our Savior and Lord. It is more than intellectual assent; it is a deep, personal reliance on Jesus's finished work on the cross and his resurrection. Union with Christ is the mysterious and profound reality that believers spiritually join Jesus through faith.

Justification is a legal declaration by God where he forgives our sins and counts us as righteous because of Jesus's righteousness. This gracious act is received by faith alone, not by our works. Justification assures us of our right to stand before God and frees us from the guilt of sin. Sanctification is the ongoing process by which the Holy Spirit transforms believers into the likeness of Jesus. Glorification is the final stage of salvation, where believers fully conform to Christ's image, with glorified bodies, free from sin and death at Christ's return.

Salvation by the Spirit is a comprehensive work of God that begins with repentance and faith, progresses through our union with Christ, justification, and sanctification, and culminates in glorification. It is a journey marked by the Spirit's presence and power, ensuring that what God has begun in us will be completed on the day of Christ Jesus.

QUESTION 31

What Is Repentance?

ANSWER

Repentance is not merely regret over sin's consequences or our failure to live up to our standards. Repentance is turning away from evil—seeing sin in light of God's holiness and experiencing conviction in response to his kindness.

THE WORLD LOVES THE IDEA of a turn-around when it means calling someone else to account for their sins. We get a little squeamish when it's someone calling us out for something *we* have done! Because we live in a world that assumes God doesn't exist or is irrelevant, we have no ultimate standard or moral basis for judging who is right or who is wrong in cultural conflict. We feel the need for restitution to be made and justice to be served, but since everyone makes up their own standards for what is right or wrong, we're left without resources when a real turn-around is necessary.

The Bible gives us a word—a category, an action—that supplies us with something much more profound than anything our society can offer: *repentance*. This admittedly churchy word may recall images of the street prophet holding signs that say, "Repent or die!" But, biblically speaking, repentance is a beautiful concept that goes far beyond what we see in the world.

Repentance is not simply saying "my bad" when we mess up. It is not merely a feeling of sorrow or regret over the consequences of sin. True repentance is the response when the human heart is exposed to the light of God's holiness and awestruck at God's undeserved kindness. Convicted of sin, we turn from wrongdoing and trade our agendas for the kingdom agenda of Jesus Christ.

The apostle Paul's testimony before King Agrippa (Acts 26:12-23) shows us how repentance works itself out in our lives. First, repentance is turning from darkness to light (Acts 26:18). Before we came to Jesus, we were moving around in this dark world, unable to see the beauty of the gospel and unwilling to accept the light. Once we repent, we turn from darkness to light.

Second, repentance is turning from Satan to God (Acts 26:18, 20). It's about switching kingdoms. Just as a person applying for citizenship in one country usually renounces their former citizenship, we pledge allegiance to King Jesus and renounce Satan and his power.

Third, repentance bears fruit in works of righteousness (Acts 26:18, 20, 23). We don't just turn from sin; we turn toward righteousness. It's not just about stopping what's bad, but starting what's good. Seen in this light, repentance as a turn-around may begin in a moment, but its effects are lifelong.

Some people think living a life of repentance means being sin-free and totally victorious over our sins and struggles. The biblical picture is different: the battle is ongoing, so repentance is not something we do just once, but a way of life. The first of Martin Luther's 95 Theses put it this way: "When our Lord and Master Jesus Christ said, 'Repent,' he willed the entire life of believers to be one of repentance."[1]

In a world bereft of forgiveness, with moralistic judgments issued in every direction based on movable standards, the Christian understanding of repentance feels refreshing, giving us hope of renewal, cleansing, and life transformation.

REFLECTION QUESTIONS

1. **Describe the signs of genuine repentance. How is repentance different from feeling regret or sorrow?** Reflect on your understanding of repentance. Consider specific instances where you may have felt regret or grief but didn't experience true repentance. How can you differentiate between these emotions and genuine repentance?

2. **How does the holiness of God influence your understanding and experience of repentance?** Think about the nature of God's holiness and how it highlights the severity of sin. How does this understanding lead you to a more profound conviction and a genuine turning away from sin?

3. **How can you trade your agendas for the kingdom agenda of Jesus Christ? What practical steps might that involve?** Examine your daily life and priorities. Identify areas where your ambitions might conflict with Jesus's teachings and mission. What changes can you make to align more closely with the kingdom agenda of Jesus Christ?

SCRIPTURE REFERENCES

- Psalm 51:10-12
- Isaiah 55:7
- Ezekiel 18:30-32
- Joel 2:13
- Matthew 3:8
- Luke 13:3
  Luke 15:7
- Acts 3:19
- Romans 2:4
- 2 Corinthians 7:10
- James 4:8-10
- 1 John 1:9

QUESTION 32

What Is Faith?

ANSWER

Faith is not based on our sincerity or the strength of our feelings; it is not believing in ourselves. Faith is accepting the truth of the gospel and entrusting ourselves to King Jesus alone.

"I'M A PERSON OF FAITH." In a previous era, this statement would be synonymous with saying "I adhere to a religious faith and follow its teachings." Today, faith is often reduced to a vague or sentimental feeling, like saying "I have a spiritual side." We talk about "believing in yourself" or "having faith" that everything will work out. It's not so important *what* you believe, just *that* you believe in something bigger than yourself. Faith becomes just a feeling, something that helps you through the day. It's something you muster up from within yourself.

What's more, because of the influence of the Enlightenment, people often think of faith and reason as opposites, as if some people rely on a leap of faith in how they see the world while others are driven solely by science and facts. The reality is more complicated: we are all people of faith. It's impossible to reason at all unless we take "on faith" certain fundamental ideas about the world and trust them to be true. (Even those who say "trust the science," by that very phrase, acknowledge there's *trust* involved!)

In the past, most people looked outside themselves to discover what was true about the world and then conformed their lives to reality. Today, we are told to look inside ourselves to find the truth. Increasingly, we seek to conform the outside world to our inner understanding of what is true and accurate.

The Bible's understanding of faith is different. It refers first to belief in the gospel, a truth that comes from outside ourselves. We hear the good news of Jesus and his life, death, and resurrection, and we assent to the truthfulness of this testimony. We confess Jesus as Lord. Biblical faith also refers to personal and total trust in God. What matters most isn't the amount of faith we have or how sincere we are about our beliefs; what matters is that the one we're putting our faith in is worthy of our trust. It's *entrusting* ourselves to Jesus the Savior and King. It's dependence not on oneself, but on Jesus as the one who brings salvation through his work.

When Christians urge others to believe, we are not advocating a religious hobby. Nor are we talking about a personal spiritual experience, as wonderful and powerful as that may be. We are proclaiming something objectively true—the crucified Jesus of Nazareth is the Messiah of Israel and the King of the world—and calling people to acknowledge this truth and bring their lives in line with this reality. We're also calling people to renounce any hope of salvation that would come from within and to receive the grace of God that comes from above. Believing in Jesus means more than just assenting to the fact he was raised from the dead. It includes a heartfelt trust in him alone for salvation, a personal relationship that leads to a transformed life.

REFLECTION QUESTIONS

1. **How would you distinguish biblical faith from believing in yourself or the power of positive thinking?** Reflect on the differences between trusting in Jesus and relying on self-confidence or optimism. How does placing your faith in Jesus provide a more solid foundation for your life?

2. **In what ways have you seen people placing their faith in faith itself or relying on their sincerity for salvation? How does this contrast with genuine faith in Jesus?** Consider examples where faith is treated as a mere feeling or a personal effort. How does this

differ from the biblical teaching that faith is a trust in Jesus's work on our behalf?

3. **How does biblical faith differ from a mere intellectual acceptance of truths about Jesus? How can you grow in the heartfelt trust that characterizes authentic faith?** Reflect on the distinction between knowing facts about Jesus and truly trusting him with your life. What practical steps can you take to deepen your relationship with him?

SCRIPTURE REFERENCES

- Mark 9:24
  Mark 11:22-24
- John 3:16
  John 14:1
- Romans 10:17
- 2 Corinthians 5:7
- Galatians 2:20
- Ephesians 2:8-9
- Hebrews 11:1
- James 2:17
- 1 Peter 1:8-9

QUESTION 33
What Is Union with Christ?

ANSWER

Union with Christ is our participation in the life, death, resurrection, and ascension of Jesus. Because Christ is in us, and we are in Christ, our identity is defined by our relationship with him.

MANY PEOPLE TODAY GROUND THEIR sense of identity in personal affiliations, career advancement, political ideologies, or social status. Worth and purpose derive from these outside measures of success, or from the internal drive to achieve results, acquire more possessions, or make of life whatever we want.

The problem with finding your identity according to these worldly markers is that they can so easily change. They fluctuate. If you base your worth and value in fleeting things, you won't have a foundation sturdy and substantial enough to stand on when suffering shows up, or when death threatens all you love.

The New Testament provides a different source of identity—a profound connection to Jesus Christ. Union with Christ is our participation in Jesus's life, death, burial, resurrection, and ascension. Because of our union with Christ, we are defined not by the marks of this world, but by the maker of this world. Not by human success, but by a divine Savior. Not by our story, but by our envelopment into his story.

The New Testament claims that those who belong to Jesus are so intertwined with him that we died when he died. "You have died, and your life is hidden with Christ in God" (Colossians 3:3). When we are united to Christ in faith, we are united with him in all he has done for us. He represents us so thoroughly that we have been "crucified with Christ" (Galatians 2:20), "buried with him" (Romans 6:4), and "raised with Christ" (Colossians 3:1). We are even "seated…with him in the heavens" (Ephesians 2:6).

We've been crucified with Christ, the apostle Paul tells us, and therefore we no longer live, but Christ lives in us (Galatians 2:20). Notice the verb tense here; it refers to a past occurrence with an enduring impact in the present. How all this works is a profound mystery. The Reformation theologian John Calvin once remarked, "For my part, I am overwhelmed by the depth of this mystery, and am not ashamed to join Paul in acknowledging at once my ignorance and my admiration...Whatever is supernatural is clearly beyond our comprehension. Let us, therefore, labor more to feel Christ living in us than to discover the nature of that intercourse."[1]

Union with Christ eliminates the need for continual self-validation. The frantic efforts to find or fabricate an acceptable identity, or the ceaseless endeavors to regulate your reputation, are never over and never done. Union with Christ means you can now rest. When God looks at you, he sees you in Christ. This is an objective reality.

But union with Christ brings about something even more marvelous: *communion* with Christ, which means we are in Christ and Christ is in us, and we are able to lean into and experience the reality of fellowship with him. He fills, illuminates, and energizes us. We can draw close to him because he draws near to us and makes his presence known.

Having Christ in us means that as we work out our salvation in fear and trembling, we know he is the one working in and through us to bear fruit in this world (Philippians 2:12). Jesus amplifies your authenticity *and* your conformity to him, making you more yourself as you become more like him. You are united with Christ, in service to the world for the glory of God.

REFLECTION QUESTIONS

1. **How has modern culture shaped your understanding of identity? Do you find yourself defining your worth through external affiliations or achievements?** Reflect on the influences that shape your sense of self-worth. How do societal norms and personal achievements impact your identity, and how can union with Christ provide a deeper, more stable foundation?

2. **In what ways does the concept of union with Christ challenge the prevalent secular notion of identity? How does it redefine how we perceive ourselves?** Consider how being united with Christ offers a different perspective on identity than the secular focus on self-reliance and external validation. How does this union transform your understanding of who you are?

3. **What are some practices that can help you experience the reality of your union with Christ?** Reflect on how union with Christ leads to communion with him. How can we draw close to Jesus, trusting his goodness as he draws near to us? What does experiencing fellowship with Jesus look like?

SCRIPTURE REFERENCES

- John 14:23
  John 15:1-5
  John 17:20-23
- Romans 6:1-11
  Romans 12:4-5
- 1 Corinthians 6:17
  1 Corinthians 12:12-27
- Galatians 2:20
  Galatians 3:28
- Ephesians 1:3-14
  Ephesians 2:4-7
  Ephesians 3:14-17
- Colossians 1:27
  Colossians 2:12-13
  Colossians 3:1-5
- 2 Peter 1:4

QUESTION 34

What Is Justification?

ANSWER

Justification is God's declaration of righteousness for all who are united to Christ through faith: his life, death, and resurrection are counted as ours. We do not earn our entry into the family of God but stand before him faultless, by faith alone.

THE DEFAULT SETTING OF THE human heart is moralism. It's the idea that good people deserve good and bad people deserve bad, and if we can just be good enough, we'll be seen to be in the right—by ourselves, by others, or by God. No wonder then that many people see religion as being primarily about moral goodness and improving our behavior. It's another way we try to be good enough. Or it's a way of bargaining with God, keeping a list of rules so he is obligated to bless us.

Moralism flows into self-justification. We all want to justify ourselves, to show that through our efforts, we've become worthy of all the good we hope to receive in life. That's why, whenever we are confronted with our failures and flaws, we try to compensate by doing enough good things to outweigh the bad. We divert attention away from our sin and toward our successes, or we make excuses for our sins and expect God to overlook our past regrets.

The problem with self-justification is that it doesn't work. Cultures shift over time regarding what is morally desirable. Societies change perspective on what achievements are most important. Besides, all our good works eventually feel like trying to cover ourselves with fig leaves. We still feel vulnerable. We can't find validation in all our good deeds because our guilt and shame are too powerful.

The Bible gives us a radically different picture of justification. Instead of self-justification, we are introduced to God's justification. We are declared to be in the right not by any good works or moral righteousness of our own, but by the free grace of God as we believe in Jesus Christ. Through faith in Jesus, we are united to him and grafted into his people, and this changes everything.

Justification cuts across the grain in a culture that seeks to prop up and promote the self at all costs. We do not set the standards of sin and righteousness—only God does. Justification is God's pronouncement that we are righteous in his eyes. It is not based on our efforts but on his grace (Romans 3:24). Not our goodness, but Christ's. This is the "great exchange" spoken of by the Reformers: Christ took our sin and clothed us in his righteousness (2 Corinthians 5:21).

Today, people pay to be admitted into clubs, memberships, and fellowships. The Christian life doesn't work like that. We can't earn our membership in God's family; our belonging comes to us as a gift, so there's no room to boast. Our acceptance into God's family is not based on our efforts, achievements, pedigree, ethnicity, or moral goodness. It's a gift freely given to us through Christ's work (Ephesians 2:8-9).

In our world, we are told that we must earn everything. Our natural state is inclined toward gaining prestige and protecting our position. The New Testament pierces through the fog with glorious news: we stand before God without fault or guilt through justification. Christ's righteousness covers our sins (Colossians 1:22).

REFLECTION QUESTIONS

1. **How does the concept of justification counter the idea of self-justification through accomplishments or moralism?** Reflect on ways you may have tried to earn validation or self-worth through your actions or achievements. How does understanding justification by faith alone change your approach to self-worth and acceptance?

2. **How does the doctrine of justification by faith alone challenge the common tendency to earn approval or validation through works?** Consider the implications of receiving God's approval as a gift

rather than something to be earned. How does this truth influence your daily life and interactions with others?

3. **Reflect on the phrase "stand before God faultless by faith alone." How does this impact your perspective on your relationship with God?** Think about how this assurance of being faultless before God affects your view of yourself and your relationship with him. How does it provide comfort, security, and motivation in your faith journey?

SCRIPTURE REFERENCES

- Romans 3:24
Romans 5:1, 9
Romans 8:33-34
Romans 10:4
- 2 Corinthians 5:21
- Galatians 2:16
- Ephesians 2:8-9
- Philippians 3:9
- Colossians 1:22
- Titus 3:5-7

QUESTION 35

What Is Sanctification?

ANSWER

Sanctification is the work of the Spirit to make us more and more like Jesus. It is not the pursuit of just being yourself but the project of growing with others in the righteousness God imparts to his people.

IN THE PAST FEW DECADES, multiple books, projects, apps, and plans have developed around accepting yourself and expecting more for yourself. The goal is to find identity through individuality. One of the main themes is that individuals seek their sense of belonging and significance through personal accomplishments.

We see the mentality of "working on yourself" everywhere we turn. The wellness industry markets self-improvement products, diets, and practices that promise physical and mental wellbeing. The corporate world often encourages employees to build personal brands, reinforcing that personal success means professional success. The advent of social media has exacerbated the pressure to present an idealized version of ourselves online, leading to comparison, envy, and a constant obsession for validation. Platforms like Instagram and TikTok perpetuate curated personas, cultivating a culture where personal image is paramount.

The Bible affirms this deep desire to become the best version of oneself but subverts the world's way of getting there. It's the Christian doctrine of sanctification that shows us how true and lasting betterment takes place.

Sanctification refers to the process of being made holy, or more specifically, becoming more like Jesus. It is God's project of remaking us, a process guided by the Holy Spirit. It's about being transformed from within, reflecting the character of Jesus Christ more and more as we are remade in his image. And it's not an isolated endeavor but a journey shared by other followers of Jesus, growing together in the righteousness God graciously imparts.

Self-improvement routines often rely on personal effort and hard work, which can lead to burnout and disappointment when change doesn't happen. Christian sanctification is grounded in God's grace and responds to his love. In a world that whispers, "Be your best self," sanctification invites you to embrace your future self—to lean forward into that perfected version of yourself God always intended and has promised to bring about.

Sanctification focuses on heart change. When we try to better ourselves in our own power, we usually make only surface-level alterations, driven by a comparison culture and superficial trends. Christian sanctification involves a profound inner transformation the Holy Spirit initiates in our lives. We want to see our attitudes and motives changed, so our outward behaviors will follow. But one way the Spirit shapes our attitudes and motives is by leading us to practices that help us abide in Jesus, so our hearts, over time, are brought in line with the disciplines we've incorporated into our lives.

Sanctification is not an individual effort. It involves community and connection. Focusing on ourselves can foster isolation and competition as we constantly compare our stature to others'. Christian sanctification happens within a community of people who know we are imperfect and depend on God's grace for change. As followers of Jesus grow in our experience of this grace, we grow in love, supporting and encouraging others rather than competing with them.

Sanctification operates with an eternal perspective. Pursuing the ideal self is limited to this temporal life and leaves individuals unsatisfied even if they achieve their goals. Christian sanctification is motivated by an eternal perspective and focuses on glorifying God and participating in his plan. Paradoxically, the self is improved precisely in getting the attention off the self and onto the unchanging, loving grace God shows through Jesus Christ.

REFLECTION QUESTIONS

1. **How has pursuing your "best self" affected your spiritual journey in a world urging us to shape our image?** Reflect on how the pursuit of self-improvement has influenced your spiritual life. Consider the changes that might occur when you focus on becoming more like Jesus rather than achieving a self-defined ideal.

2. **Consider the role of community in your growth. How has walking alongside others enriched your understanding of sanctification?** Think about the impact of community involvement on your spiritual growth. How have the experiences and development of others in your community inspired and encouraged your journey of sanctification?

3. **Think about the areas where you've been striving to become your best self in your own power. How can sanctification invite you to surrender those ambitions to the shaping hands of the Spirit?** Identify the areas in your life where you've focused on self-improvement. How can you shift your efforts to align with the work of the Holy Spirit in transforming you into the likeness of Christ?

SCRIPTURE REFERENCES

- John 17:17
- Romans 6:22
Romans 12:2
- 2 Corinthians 3:18
2 Corinthians 5:17
- Galatians 5:22-23
- Ephesians 4:22-24
- Philippians 1:6
Philippians 2:12-13
- Colossians 3:10
- 1 Thessalonians 4:3-4
- 2 Thessalonians 2:13
- Hebrews 10:14
- 1 Peter 1:14-16
- 1 John 3:2-3

QUESTION 36

What Is Glorification?

ANSWER

Glorification is the Spirit's ultimate work, resurrecting us into eternal splendor as we are fully transformed into the likeness of Jesus. Our hope for immortality rests in God's promise, not human plans.

"WHAT IT MEANS TO BE human, from our brains and bodies to our values and ways of life, is 'poised to be transformed' as we move from a 'purely biological species' to a 'techno-human hybrid'. It's a very different kind of trans debate."[1] So writes Samuel Fishwick in *The Standard,* capturing the newest quest for immortality through human ingenuity.

Transhumanism promises we can transcend our limitations and achieve physical immortality through technology. This promise has led to investments in cryonics, experimental procedures, and life-extension technologies, all as an attempt to secure a longer life on our terms. The vision is for us to become our own saviors.

In contrast, the Christian understanding of glorification shatters the illusions of human self-sufficiency. It redirects our gaze to God's unchanging promises. It fulfills the desire for everlasting life, but in a different way. Transhumanism seeks to conquer death; the Bible teaches that death has already been conquered and will one day be destroyed forever (1 Corinthians 15:26). God's promises assure us that through faith in Christ, we will experience transformation beyond the bounds of human innovation. We call this truth "glorification."

In glorification, the Holy Spirit completes the transformative journey he began in us. This process starts with renewing our hearts and minds through sanctification before we die (Romans 8:29). Then, glorification involves a resurrection after our physical death. No longer subject to decay, our bodies will be resurrected in imperishable splendor (1 Corinthians 15:42-44). This transformation is not merely a continuation of our earthly existence but a new and glorious life in the body.

Glorification represents the culmination of our sanctification journey as we are perfected and fully conformed to the image of Christ (1 John 3:2). Our character, desires, and actions will align perfectly with his nature, reflecting his holiness and righteousness. This reality does not make us less ourselves, but more so, more of the persons God always created us to be.

The promise of glorification is rooted in God's unchanging faithfulness. Through faith, we look forward to realizing this promise as we eagerly await the redemption of our bodies (Romans 8:23). This hope sustains us amid life's challenges. Unlike human endeavors to attain immortality or self-enhancement, glorification is not dependent on our efforts or technological advancements. Our confidence lies in God's power and sovereignty, not our limited abilities. We can face death with defiance because we know death will not have the last word. And we can continue to make progress in our sanctification because we know, no matter how many times we fail, that God has promised to finish the work he began in us. He will complete his work.

Glorification is not about our human feats but God's faithfulness. It's about being raised imperishable by the Creator of life himself. Our hope is not found in laboratories of innovation but the empty tomb, in the power of the resurrected Christ who conquered the grave and now offers eternal life by his grace alone. Resting in God's promises grants us far more satisfying hope than any human endeavor can offer.

REFLECTION QUESTIONS

1. **How does glorification stand in contrast to the pursuit of immortality through human ingenuity?** Reflect on how the promise of glorification through the Holy Spirit differs from the vision of transhumanism and other technological pursuits for life extension. Consider what it means to place your hope in God's promises rather than in human plans.

2. **How does the hope of being transformed into the likeness of Christ shape your understanding of your life right now?** Contemplate the ongoing process of sanctification and how it prepares you for the ultimate transformation into Christ's image. Reflect on how this transformation influences your daily actions, character, and desires and how it provides hope amid life's challenges.

3. **In what ways does the assurance of glorification through God's promise provide a more satisfying and secure hope than human efforts at self-enhancement?** Consider the limitations of human knowledge and strength in achieving immortality. Reflect on the significance of God's unchanging faithfulness and the power of the Holy Spirit in securing your future resurrection and eternal life. How does this assurance impact your perspective on life and your trust in God's plan?

SCRIPTURE REFERENCES

- Romans 8:18-30
- 1 Corinthians 15:42-44
- 2 Corinthians 3:18
- Philippians 3:20-21
- Colossians 3:4
- 1 Thessalonians 4:17
- 2 Timothy 2:10
- Titus 2:13
- Hebrews 9:28
- 1 Peter 5:10
- 1 John 3:2
- Revelation 21:3-4

PART 6

The People of God

The people of God encompasses the community of believers called to live under God's reign, united by faith in Christ, and empowered by the Holy Spirit to fulfill God's purposes in the world. This section explores this redeemed community's identity, practices, and mission.

The kingdom of God is God's reign and rule inaugurated by Jesus Christ. Believers are called to seek first the kingdom, embodying its values and priorities in their daily lives. The church is the community of believers who confess Jesus Christ as Lord. It is a local and global entity, described in Scripture as the body of Christ, the bride of Christ, and the temple of the Holy Spirit. The mission of the church is to make disciples of all nations, proclaiming the gospel and demonstrating Christ's love. The church is called to be a light in the darkness, reflecting God's glory and advancing his kingdom.

Baptism showcases a believer's identification with Jesus Christ's death, burial, and resurrection. It is an outward expression of an inward reality, marking one's entrance into the covenant community of faith. The Lord's Supper, or Communion, was instituted by Jesus to remember his sacrificial death and anticipate his return. This practice fosters unity, gratitude, and a deep sense of God's presence among his people.

Worship is the adoration and devotion we offer to God. It involves individual and corporate expressions of praise, gratitude, and surrender. Worship is a response to God's greatness and grace, shaping our hearts and lives as we seek to glorify him in all we do. The people of God live out their faith in community, engaging with Scripture and in prayer, and fulfilling the church's mission of making disciples. Through worship, service, and evangelism, believers reflect God's love and glory to the world.

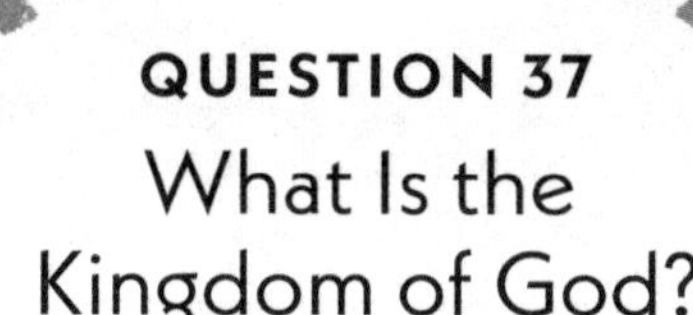

QUESTION 37

What Is the Kingdom of God?

ANSWER

The kingdom of God is the redemptive rule of God through his people over his creation—a reign already present, though not yet in fullness. We do not build the kingdom; yet by grace we are drawn into the work of God to remake the world under Jesus the King.

WE LIVE IN A CULTURE still haunted by religion, with the ghosts of religion everywhere. Postmodern philosopher Michel Foucault said religious ideas have not disappeared; they've been dispersed. One example he gives is confession, the practice of being open and honest about one's sins, either to God or to another person.[1] Even in an era of religious decline, confession hasn't disappeared; it's just moved. We see confession in therapeutic counseling, social media posts, and autobiographical writing. People still feel the need to share, but this new environment leaves us without any lasting sense of absolution.

In a similar way, certain religious impulses have gravitated toward the political realm. We are always in search of a new agenda, a new class of leaders, new laws that will enact justice and peace—some way of bringing the world in line with our vision.

The Bible offers us a vision of the world that transcends the earthly kingdoms that vie for our allegiance. All the side stories of politics—all the religious impulses that lead us to pin our hopes on contemporary leaders—get subsumed under the larger umbrella of God's promise to remake this world under King Jesus. Jesus told his followers to seek his kingdom first (Matthew 6:33). Seeking first the kingdom means more than rearranging your priorities; it implies taking on a new way of seeing everything.

According to Scripture, the kingdom of God is the redemptive rule of God through his people over his creation. Remember God's original intention for humanity to steward his creation (Genesis 1:26-28)? With Jesus the King working through his followers, we see a glimpse of God's restorative plan, involving spiritual and earthly renewal through his people. That's why Jesus instructs us to pray: "Your kingdom come, your will be done on earth as it is in heaven" (Matthew 6:10).

In the New Testament, we learn that the reign of Jesus is already present, though not yet in fullness. There is an "already, not yet" tension that characterizes the kingdom. Through Jesus's ministry, the kingdom has been inaugurated. His reign is operative in the lives of his followers (Luke 17:21). However, the kingdom's full consummation awaits Jesus's return (Revelation 11:15), when God's rule will be manifest in every corner of creation.

Sometimes Christians talk about building or bringing the kingdom, which overestimates the power of good-intentioned people to change the world for the better. Rightly understood, we don't build or bring the kingdom. Only God can do that. We do, however, work in ways God uses to extend the kingdom. We reject the utopian vision you sometimes find in political activity, and we rely on God to enact true transformation. We don't bring the kingdom, but we are invited to join God in his work of remaking the world. We cooperate with God in his redemptive plan.

Some in our day appreciate Christianity for its cultural impact. But it's not enough to want the kingdom without the King. It's not enough to enjoy the effects of Christianity without the heart. And the New Testament is clear: Jesus is King of kings and Lord of lords (Revelation 17:14). Our participation in God's kingdom work is rooted in allegiance to him.

REFLECTION QUESTIONS

1. **How does the kingdom of God challenge common notions of power and authority? What are some practical implications of acknowledging Christ as King daily?** Recognizing Christ's ultimate authority over everything changes your perspective on power and influence.

2. **In what ways can you discern the "already, but not yet" dynamic of God's kingdom in your journey of faith? How does this tension inspire hope and perseverance?** Consider moments in your life where you've seen glimpses of God's kingdom at work and how you navigate the tension between the present reality and the future fulfillment of his reign. How does this understanding encourage you to remain hopeful and steadfast in your faith journey?

3. **Reflect on the truth that we do not build the kingdom of God but are drawn into God's work by grace. How does this perspective shift your approach to Christian living and service?** Consider how viewing Christian living and service as participating in God's work by grace rather than building the kingdom ourselves changes your motivation and approach. How does this perspective influence your attitude toward serving others and engaging in God's mission?

SCRIPTURE REFERENCES

- Daniel 2:44
- Matthew 4:17
  Matthew 6:10, 33
  Matthew 13:31-32
- Mark 1:15
- Luke 17:20-21
- John 18:36
- Romans 14:17
- 1 Corinthians 4:20
- Colossians 1:13-14
- 2 Timothy 4:18
- Revelation 11:15

QUESTION 38

What Is the Church?

ANSWER

The church is the people of God—established by the gospel and chosen by grace. It is not a religious club or social action group. The church comes together to be a local embassy, a picture of God's kingdom through worship and love.

EVEN IN A TIME OF increasing isolation, people still gravitate toward clubs and groups, whether online or in person. Some people belong to the Rotary. Others to a bowling league. Fandom shows up around pop stars, celebrities, and stories. Some become members of a school association. Others get involved in a political party. It's not surprising that some would see the church in such terms—a place to get together with people who share similar interests and to make friends, or a community that can be harnessed to help bring about social and political change.

But the Bible says something different about the church. It's not a tool for our personal development. It's not a place for Bible hobbyists to quiz each other. It's not an instrument for any political agenda. The church is the people of God, grounded in a much deeper reality than voluntary association. It is the living body of Christ, founded and empowered by the Spirit of God. The church is the movement of God in the world today.

It's not uncommon for professing Christians to see the church as optional, a supplement to personal faith (seen as the *real* focus of Christianity). But the New Testament sees the church as essential to the Christian faith. We are called *out* of the world *into* the church. We are adopted into a new family. All the instructions in the letters of the New Testament take for granted that we will be in community with other believers who help us grow in spiritual maturity, so we come to look more and more like Jesus.

When believers gather, when we love and welcome each other, when we cheer each other on and hold each other accountable, when we worship God in word and deed, we demonstrate our identity as a Spirit-empowered community representing God's kingdom. The church is like a signpost in the road that points back to the cross and forward to the coming kingdom of God.

Members of the church are chosen in Jesus Christ (Ephesians 1:4-5); we are a royal priesthood and a holy nation (1 Peter 2:9). The church is the gospel made visible, founded on the confession that Jesus is the Messiah, the Son of God. Through words and works of love, the church showcases God's grace, seen in our obedience as we make disciples, baptize them, and celebrate the Lord's Supper together.

Worship is the vertical dimension of the church. Loving others is the horizontal dimension of the church. The church is like a teaser trailer for the kingdom of God as worship and love occur. It's not the whole movie. It doesn't give you all the details. But it gives you a picture of what the film will be about. Every church is an embassy—an advance outpost—of the New Jerusalem, the city God says will one day come down from heaven (Acts 2, Revelation 21:2), when heaven and earth become one.

As a holy priesthood, the church is to offer God the spiritual sacrifice of worship. As a holy nation, the church is tasked with spreading the fame of God's name through sharing the gospel and showing God's love, as a witness to his glory.

REFLECTION QUESTIONS

1. **How has your understanding of the church grown and changed over the years? Reflect on the influences that have shaped your experience.** Consider your journey in the faith and how your perception of the church has evolved. Think about the teachings, experiences, and relationships that have impacted your understanding of what it means to be part of the church.

2. **How can your church more effectively represent God's kingdom in your community?** Reflect on practical ways your church can embody corporately the values and teachings of God's kingdom.

Think about how you, as an individual, can contribute to this mission in making a meaningful impact in your community.

3. **Reflect on the idea that the church is chosen by grace and empowered by the Spirit. How does this truth shape your sense of belonging within the church? How can you extend this sense of belonging to others?** Consider ways to help others feel included and valued within your church community.

SCRIPTURE REFERENCES

- Matthew 16:18
- John 13:34-35
- Acts 2:42-47
- Romans 12:4-5
- 1 Corinthians 10:31
  1 Corinthians 12:12-14, 27
- Ephesians 2:19-22
  Ephesians 4:11-13
- Colossians 1:18
- 1 Thessalonians 5:11
- Hebrews 10:24-25
- 1 Peter 2:9-10
- Revelation 21:2-33

QUESTION 39

What Is Baptism?

ANSWER

Baptism is the public sign of our salvation—an identity marker that reveals we are not our own but belong to the people of God. Baptism signifies our purification from sin and our participation in Jesus's death and resurrection.

IDENTITY POLITICS IS AN OUTLOOK on life based on group identity. It measures life in terms of power and divides groups neatly into categories of oppressor and oppressed. In identity politics, individuals find their primary identity through various categorizations such as race, gender, nationality, social class, or religious affiliation.

There may be aspects in this way of thinking that align with what the Bible teaches regarding the pervasiveness of sin and the importance of justice in society. And yet there is something dangerously reductionistic in this ideology, a simplifying and flattening out of essential facts and distinctions. An undercurrent in identity politics leads to contradictions—"you are whatever group you belong to" *and* "you are what you make of yourself." This is where the "be true to yourself" mindset ("only you can define yourself") and identity politics ("you are defined by your group") merge: "I identify myself this way and with this group."

Baptism counters the script of identity politics just as it counters the "be true to yourself" mindset. In baptism, we see the kingdom of God as our primary source of identity and God's people as our primary place for belonging. Baptism is the initiatory sign that marks us out as belonging to Jesus and his people. When you step into those waters, you're not proclaiming, "I am what I make of myself." Instead, you're saying, "I am what God has made me to be." It's not so much "I claim Christ" as it is "Christ has claimed me."

Baptism is a spiritual bath. Just as we wash away dirt to be clean on the outside, baptism illustrates how Jesus has cleansed us from our sins on the inside (Acts 22:16). In our day, life change is often viewed as a personal, internal, and self-driven journey. But baptism points to Jesus Christ as the way to be changed. It's a reminder that our identity and transformation are inseparable from our union with him (2 Corinthians 5:17). When we go under the water during baptism, we're buried with Jesus in his death. And when we come out of the water, we rise with him in his resurrection. It's a powerful declaration that we are not our own but belong to God (Romans 6:3-4). It's also a picture of our renunciation of the Evil One and all his schemes. Baptism means our past has been buried, and our future has been reborn in Jesus Christ.

This means the most important identity marker is not our political affiliation, our ethnicity, our gender, or our class—as crucial as some of these aspects might be. Baptism tells the world we've been grafted into a more prominent people, the family of God. It's like receiving a jersey that marks you're now part of the team. We're no longer just individuals; we're part of something much bigger (1 Corinthians 12:13). We've been reborn in Christ, we've joined the fellowship of all who repent and believe (Galatians 3:28), and we move forward on mission together.

REFLECTION QUESTIONS

1. **How have you struggled with reconciling your identity in Christ through baptism with other identity stories that are popular in our culture today?** Reflect on any personal conflicts or challenges you have faced in aligning your identity as a follower of Christ with societal expectations or norms. Consider how baptism has influenced your sense of self in these situations.

2. **In a culture where identity is often linked to external factors such as wealth, fame, and appearance, how can the meaning of baptism lead us to a deeper, more authentic understanding of identity?** Contemplate the cultural pressures to define yourself by external achievements and appearances. Think about how the significance

of baptism offers a counternarrative, grounding your identity in something eternal and unchanging.

3. **How can your baptism serve as a continual reminder of your identity as a member of God's family and a participant in his kingdom?** Consider practical ways baptism can remind you of your belonging to God and your role within his kingdom. Reflect on how this perspective can influence your daily actions and interactions with others.

SCRIPTURE REFERENCES

- Matthew 3:13-17
  Matthew 28:19-20
- Mark 16:16
- Acts 2:38
  Acts 8:36-39
  Acts 10:44-48
  Acts 22:16
- Romans 6:3-4
- Galatians 3:27
- Colossians 2:12
- 1 Peter 3:21

QUESTION 40

What Is the Lord's Supper?

ANSWER

The Lord's Supper is communion with King Jesus at his table with his people. We eat the bread and drink the cup, giving thanks for his body and blood, strengthened for service by this foretaste of the feast to come.

AFTER WORLD WAR II, consumer culture took off in America. As a response to the lean years of the Great Depression and fueled by the far reach of television, the appetite for accumulating more and more possessions increased. William Leach, a professor at Columbia University, captured this season well: "The cardinal features of this culture were acquisition and consumption as the means of achieving happiness; the cult of the new; the democratization of desire; and money value as the predominant measure of all value in society."[1]

A consumer culture is not morally neutral: it trains us to see the world in specific ways. The urge to acquire and consume is often tied to feelings of unworthiness and insecurity. This relentless system fosters perpetual dissatisfaction and restlessness, urging us to seek new things to fill the void within us constantly.

The Lord's Supper addresses our spiritual hunger and profound discontentment. Here, we are brought back to the central act of grace in the universe: the Son of God's offering of his body and blood as the atoning sacrifice for our sins. The depths of our discontent can only be satisfied by the abundance of the provision of Jesus Christ for empty sinners on the cross. Christians not only consume the Lord's Supper; we are transformed in the presence of God and then sent out as part of the movement of God in the world (John 6:56). We don't lose our identities; we embrace our role within a larger body (1 Corinthians 12:12-27). The supper reminds us that the way to be complete is to empty ourselves in service of God and other people (Philippians 2:1-11).

At the heart of the Lord's Supper is our intimate communion with

Jesus our King. The supper is not a mere ritual but a spiritual encounter where we draw near to Christ. Furthermore, when we gather around the Lord's table, we take our place as part of a larger community of believers. In 1 Corinthians 10:17, Paul underscored that we who partake of the one bread are one body. It's not an individualistic act but a communal one.

In John 6:35, Jesus declared, "I am the bread of life"—he sustains and nourishes our souls. The cup is his blood—he brings forgiveness and redemption (Matthew 26:27-28). Through these elements, we feed on Christ in faith and receive sustenance for the future. We express our thankfulness for Christ's body, which was given to us, and his blood shed for the forgiveness of sins (Matthew 26:28).

The Lord's Supper isn't merely a commemoration of a past event; it's a present source of spiritual strength. As physical food nourishes our bodies, the supper empowers us spiritually. God's strengthening grace enables us to fulfill our calling to serve God and others. And each time we take the supper, we catch a glimpse of future glory. Revelation 19:9 speaks of the marriage feast of the Lamb, the ultimate union between Christ and his church. The Lord's Supper is a foretaste of our joyous eternity with him.

REFLECTION QUESTIONS

1. **How do you see consumer culture impacting people's desires and needs? How does the Lord's Supper offer an alternative perspective?** Reflect on the influence of consumerism in your own life. Consider how the Lord's Supper, focusing on spiritual nourishment and community, provides a counternarrative to the consumerist mindset.

2. **How does partaking in the Lord's Supper with fellow believers deepen your sense of community and belonging within the church?** Think about your experiences during the Lord's Supper and how they have shaped your relationship with other believers.

Explore the significance of sharing the Lord's Supper as the unified body of Christ.

3. **In what ways has participating in the Lord's Supper strengthened your spiritual life and service to others?** Reflect on specific instances where the Lord's Supper has provided spiritual strength and motivation for serving others. Consider how this practice has influenced your actions and attitudes toward service.

SCRIPTURE REFERENCES

- Matthew 6:31-33
- Mark 14:22-24
- Luke 14:15
  Luke 22:19-20
- John 6:53-56
- 1 Corinthians 10:16-17
  1 Corinthians 11:23-30
- Philippians 2:3-4
  Philippians 4:11-13
- 1 Peter 1:18-19
- Revelation 19:9

QUESTION 41

What Is the Bible?

ANSWER

The Bible is God's inspired Word that tells the story of the world and testifies to King Jesus. It is our supreme authority in faith and practice. God's Word is not a textbook we master but a world we inhabit, where we encounter the Divine Author who changes us.

"THE BIBLE IS JUST A religious text, full of myths and fables, a tool for judgment and condemnation." So goes the thinking among many people today when they consider the Bible and its impact on society. But even among those who disbelieve the Bible, you will often find a begrudging respect for its breathtaking literary beauty, or the sheer impact this book has had and continues to have on the world.

Christianity's view of the Bible places it in another category from all other books. We believe the Bible is the Spirit-breathed Word of God. The Holy Spirit worked through human authors to communicate God's message to humanity. It's a divine-human collaboration where God's wisdom and truth are perfectly expressed through people's words.

The Bible is the true story of the whole world. It lays out the grand narrative of creation, fall, redemption, and restoration. Authors of the Bible include kings, peasants, philosophers, fishermen, poets, politicians, and scholars. The books of the Bible cover history, sermons, letters, songs, and love poetry. There are geographical surveys, architectural specifications, travel diaries, population statistics, family trees, inventories, and numerous legal documents. In all, the Bible bears witness to Jesus Christ, the focus of divine revelation (John 5:39). Every story culminates in the life, teachings, death, burial, resurrection, and ascension of Jesus.

Unlike a text you would study in hopes of mastering its contents, the Bible is a story we inhabit. The Bible is to form, norm, and narrate our lives. It is the supreme guide in determining what we believe and how we should live. It reveals principles and values that undergird our beliefs and actions. James 1:22 encourages us not to be "hearers only" but "doers of the word," meaning we should put into practice its precepts. The Bible becomes the spectacles we look through to see and make sense of the world.

The Bible's primary message focuses on redemption, reconciliation, and God's love for the world through Jesus Christ. Further, the Bible harmonizes the themes of justice and mercy. Most centrally, at the cross of Jesus Christ, we see the coming together of love and justice as Jesus died in the place of guilty sinners. Instead of using the Bible as a tool for condemning others, we should note its encouragement toward self-examination (2 Corinthians 13:5) and its warnings of self-deception. The Bible addresses sin and its consequences while offering hope and love.

When we read the Bible, we are engaged in a practice that goes beyond the reading of mere words. In these pages, we encounter the Divine Author himself as we read. Through the Bible, God reveals his will and his truth, inviting us into relationship with him.

REFLECTION QUESTIONS

1. **How has understanding the Bible as the narrative of God's interaction with humanity shaped your perspective on history, purpose, and your place in the world?** Reflect on how viewing the Bible as a comprehensive story changes your understanding of your life and purpose within the larger context of God's plan.

2. **In what ways does recognizing that all the Scriptures point to Jesus help you read individual Bible stories?** Consider how seeing Jesus as the central figure of the Bible influences how you read

Scripture, how you view his role in your life, and how you respond to his authority.

3. **Can you recall a time when, while reading the Bible, it felt like you were encountering God personally? What did that experience teach you about your relationship with God?** Consider specific moments when the Bible seemed to speak directly to you and explore what these experiences reveal about your connection to God and his Word.

SCRIPTURE REFERENCES

- Joshua 1:8
- Psalm 1:1-3
  Psalm 19:7-8
  Psalm 119:105
- Isaiah 40:8
- Matthew 4:4
- John 1:1-2
  John 5:39
- Acts 17:11
- Romans 15:4
- 2 Timothy 3:16-17
- Hebrews 4:12

QUESTION 42
What Is Prayer?

ANSWER

Prayer is communion with God in the name of the Son with the help of the Spirit. Prayer is a pursuit not of "mindfulness" but the mind of Jesus, through praise, confession, and petition. Its aim is not self-expression, but spiritual formation.

IN A TIME OF WIDESPREAD anxiety and mental distress, it's not surprising to see people pursuing practices and habits that promise peace and solace. Mindfulness routines have arisen in recent years, often rooted in Eastern philosophies, primarily Buddhism, which involve intentional, nonjudgmental awareness of the present moment. Practitioners often focus on their breath, bodily sensations, or sensory experiences to cultivate this awareness.

There may be therapeutic benefits to mindfulness practices, but by beginning with self, mindfulness routines turn us inward, to our own thoughts and feelings, rather than upward to God in a spirit of devotion, or outward to others in acts of justice and mercy. Christian prayer incorporates what is best about these mindfulness efforts while overcoming their shortcomings.

Christian prayer is not emptying the mind of distraction but filling the mind with truth—God's promises, seen most clearly in the character and the redemptive work of Christ. Prayer is a crucial way we become like Jesus, where our inner person is gradually reshaped to conform to his mind and attitude. Christian prayer is not just about self-awareness but Christ-awareness. In prayer, we don't just observe our mental landscape; we experience a divine makeover where our thoughts, desires, and perspectives are reshaped.

The Bible's vision of prayer is profoundly personal. It's not just a monologue, where we speak our thoughts into silence; it's a dialogue, a heartfelt conversation with God, an openness to receive and respond to his Word. Prayer is an invitation to present yourself before God in all your mess, with all your doubts, with all your frustrations, and to trust that the God who knows you still loves you. It's to draw near like a child, and to unburden yourself in God's presence. It's dwelling with God.

Praying in the name of Jesus is more than attaching his name to the end of our requests; it's our humble confession that we need a mediator. We don't have the status or standing to approach God on our own; we rely on the Son's merit to enter the Father's throne room.

The Holy Spirit is our guide in prayer (Romans 8:26). Life sometimes feels like walking an uncharted path in the dark. The Spirit in prayer functions as a guide who brings light and direction to the journey. He's also a skilled translator who perfectly translates our hearts' groans and sighs to the Father.

Three aspects of prayer form a harmonious symphony. Praise magnifies God's glory, confession deepens our intimacy, and petition reinforces our reliance on his wisdom and care. Praise is when the magnitude of God's beauty and awesomeness overwhelms us. It is an eruption of the soul's delight. Confession is when we realize how far we've missed the mark and want to be forgiven. Petition is when we share our desires, concerns, and needs with God.

Christian prayer offers a different perspective in a world that often encourages self-expression as the best way to find peace. Spiritual formation is about the Spirit's work to align the self with God's purposes. It's his work in and through us, not our own. Through prayer, we surrender to the need to be the author of our stories and yield to God's leading in our lives.

REFLECTION QUESTIONS

1. **What is the primary purpose of prayer in your life? Is it more about self-expression or spiritual formation?** Reflect on your motivations for praying and consider how to shift your focus toward spiritual formation, depending on the Spirit to align your heart and mind with God's will.

2. **What are some ways to ask for God's guidance during prayer? What practices have you found helpful in learning to pray?** Consider the balance between speaking and listening in your prayer life and explore ways to deepen your experience of God's guidance through prayer.

3. **How does prayer help you align your desires and thoughts with God's will? Are there areas in your life where you struggle with this alignment?** Reflect on how prayer shapes your desires and thoughts to align with God's purposes and identify areas where you seek greater alignment with his will.

SCRIPTURE REFERENCES

- Psalm 145:18
- Jeremiah 29:12
- Matthew 6:9-13
- John 14:13-14
- Romans 8:26
Romans 12:2
- Philippians 2:5
Philippians 4:6-7
- Colossians 4:2
- 1 Thessalonians 5:16-18
- James 5:16
- 1 John 1:9
1 John 5:14

QUESTION 43

What Is the Mission of the Church?

ANSWER

The mission of the church is to make disciples of King Jesus by declaring the gospel and displaying its power. The church is not a club, a charity, or a source of prosperity. In the power of the Spirit, we follow and obey King Jesus for the glory of God and the good of the world.

BUSINESSES HAVE MISSION STATEMENTS. Politicians have mission statements. Charitable organizations have mission statements. These statements explain why institutions exist, or what drives and motivates the people who take part. The church has a mission also (or as some theologians have said, God's mission has a church!), and it's easy for others to conceive of the church's primary task as falling into the same category as other organizations with mission statements.

Some see the church as just another exclusive group focused on rituals and traditions with little attention to what is taking place in the outside world. It's true the church is organized with appointed leaders and systems and structures. But this view fails to capture the vibrant, transformative work the church is all about. Unlike clubs with a mission statement, the church *is* mission. Its impact extends beyond its walls into the world, seeking to bring hope, healing, and reconciliation.

Others see the church as a social action group involved in works of charity. While the church is undoubtedly involved in social action and justice, reducing its involvement with the world to humanitarian work overlooks the core message of the gospel and discipleship. The church lives according to the command of God to "act justly, to love faithfulness, and to walk humbly with your God" (Micah 6:8). This means more than the typical humanitarian effort; this is the expression of compassionate neighbor-love that flows from the gospel of Jesus Christ. The church's goal is to make disciples who receive the transformative love of God and become agents of change.

More than a few people these days look at the church as a source of personal prosperity. Go to church and God will make you rich! Some see the church as a way to increase status and prosperity by tapping into divine power to grant wealth or fulfillment. This perspective misses the communal and selfless nature of the church. The abundant life promised by Jesus is not a life of wealth and possessions but a life of joy through self-giving love.

What does the church do, then? We make disciples. That means, first and foremost, in the power of the Spirit, we call everyone everywhere to ongoing repentance and faith. We are witnesses to King Jesus, messengers of his kingdom. Second, we demonstrate the power of the gospel in how we live. We are transformed into salt and light (Matthew 5:13-16), so the world may taste and see that the Lord is good (Psalm 34:8).

The church exists for the glory of God and the good of the world. We love God and neighbor. We are sent into the world as the Father has sent the Son (John 20:21). As God's people, we serve the world around us by delivering the gospel message uncompromised, and by living according to the gospel in ways that magnify the God of grace.

REFLECTION QUESTIONS

1. **How do you engage in the church's mission of making disciples, and what challenges have you faced in this pursuit?** Reflect on your involvement in disciple-making and identify any obstacles you've encountered. Consider how you can overcome these challenges and more effectively contribute to the church's mission.

2. **In what ways have you been involved in initiatives that seek the good of your community and the world? How do these efforts align with the church's mission?** Think about your participation in serving the world around you. Assess how these efforts align with

the church's mission and how you can enhance your impact for the glory of God and the good of the world.

3. **What does it mean for you to live under the Lordship of Christ, both personally and in your interactions with the world around you?** Explore the implications of Christ's Lordship in your life. Reflect on how you can embody this commitment in daily interactions and influence others through your example.

SCRIPTURE REFERENCES

- Matthew 28:19-20
- John 20:21
- Acts 1:8
- Romans 1:16
  Romans 10:14-15
- 2 Corinthians 5:20-21
- Ephesians 3:20-21
  Ephesians 4:11-13
- Philippians 2:15-16
- Colossians 1:28
  Colossians 3:17
- James 1:21-22
- 1 Peter 2:9
- 1 John 1:9

QUESTION 44

Why Do We Tell People About Jesus?

ANSWER

We tell others about Jesus because of love: love for God who gave his only Son as the only Savior, love for our neighbors whose salvation we desire, and love for the gospel that reveals the truth about our world.

"EVANGELISM IS NOT PRIMARILY ABOUT selling products and services; it's about sharing what you love and believe."[1] Those are the words of Guy Kawasaki, the chief evangelist of Canva, former evangelist of Apple. Today's world often sees influential figures and celebrities acting as brand ambassadors. They are passionate about certain products or services, using their fame and charisma to persuade others to follow their lead. Brand evangelists love a product so much they can't help but talk about it with others.

While the concept of brand ambassadors is prevalent in marketing, it differs significantly from sharing the message of Jesus. Brand evangelists often get involved in marketing in part because of their desire for personal gain or popularity. But Christians don't market the gospel, because the gospel is not a product. Christians announce the gospel, because the gospel is *news.* And the motivation for sharing this news is a genuine love for God and love for our neighbors. We're not promoting a brand of church or Christianity; we're proclaiming the message of salvation from sin and death.

The "why" behind our mission to tell others about Jesus can be distilled into a single word: *Love.* Love is the driving force, the engine of motivation, that propels us to engage in sharing the message of Christ with the world. Love is the heartbeat of evangelism—sharing the gospel. We are not driven by fear, insecurity, or coercion. We are on a mission motivated by love—love for God, love for our neighbors, and love for the gospel. This love compels us to share the most precious gift we've ever received: salvation by grace through faith in Jesus Christ.

Our love for God, who gave his only Son as the only Savior, is the deepest motivation for our mission. John 3:16 is the cornerstone we build on. Our love for the world is only possible because God loved the world first and sent his Son to be the Savior.

As we grow in our love for God, we naturally grow in our love and compassion for our neighbors. Our actions aren't rooted in judgment or condemnation, but in a sincere desire for the wellbeing of others, both in this life and for eternity. We share God's heart that all would come to repentance. We recognize that apart from Jesus, people face the peril of spiritual separation from God. There is no other name under heaven by which humanity can be saved (Acts 4:12). Our mission is not merely a religious duty but a heartfelt response, grounded in the love of God himself and his concern for humanity. Evangelism flows from compassion, just as God's desire for people everywhere to turn from sin and turn to him in faith flows from his compassionate nature.

Our love for the gospel is grounded in the reality that we are not just delivering a simple message; we're handling dynamite. We know the gospel to be the dynamic power of God for salvation. We know the gospel tells the explosive truth about our world. We love the gospel because we've seen how powerful it is when the Spirit applies it to human hearts. We believe the gospel can transform broken lives, offer hope to the hopeless, and heal the wounded. Love: this is why we share the good news of Jesus.

REFLECTION QUESTIONS

1. **What are some loveless motivations that may lead people to share the gospel, and how would love make a difference?** Reflect on your motivations for evangelism. Consider how love for God, love for your neighbors, and love for the gospel motivate you to share the message of Jesus with others.

2. **Can you share a story of when you talked about Jesus with someone?** Think about a specific experience where you shared the gospel with someone. Reflect on how the conversation went, what you learned from it, and how it shaped you and the person you shared with.

3. **What are some practical ways you can talk more about Jesus in your everyday routines?** Consider how you can demonstrate love for God and your neighbors through everyday actions. Consider specific ways to integrate evangelism into your daily life and interactions with others.

SCRIPTURE REFERENCES

- Matthew 5:14-16
  Matthew 22:37-39
- Mark 16:15
- John 3:16
- Acts 1:8
- Romans 1:16
  Romans 10:14-15
- 1 Corinthians 13:2
- 2 Corinthians 5:14
- Colossians 3:14
- 1 Peter 3:15
- 2 Peter 3:9
- 1 John 4:19

QUESTION 45

Why Do We Love and Serve Our Neighbors?

ANSWER

We love and serve our neighbors as a sign of the kingdom of God. We do good works not to prove our goodness or earn salvation, but as the overflow of God's love working in and through us.

IN OUR WORLD TODAY, some view good works of justice or involvement in social action as a way of demonstrating their identity as a good person or a way of earning favor with God. Good works help us feel better about ourselves or prove our moral standing and worthiness. We want to feel validated and righteous, and the acts of kindness we perform for our neighbors, or our participation in the political process, or our charitable activities—all these can help us stand out.

The problem with this kind of love and service is that it doesn't escape the trap of self-centeredness. If the good things we do are merely about proving ourselves, or earning favor with God so he will give us blessings, or securing a heavenly afterlife, all our good deeds are *really,* deep down, selfish. They're all about us.

The Bible's view of love and service is different. Because salvation comes as a gift of God's grace, our good works are free to flow from a heart transformed by God's love. Instead of seeking validation, we perform good works because we've already been loved and accepted by God (2 Corinthians 9:11). We are freed to truly love and serve our neighbors—not with the selfish impulse of seeking our own good, but with sincerity, caring for their wellbeing above all else.

Many today get on board with any attempt to pursue justice in society (however loosely justice might be defined). And, of course, we celebrate the societal benefits when people pursue justice and do good to others. But the Bible goes further in recognizing a profound spiritual purpose in our love and service. Good works are more than displays of human kindness; they are demonstrations of God's love. Our pursuit of justice is more than making the world a better place; it reflects the righteous character of God. When we seek justice and love mercy, we offer a foretaste of God's coming kingdom, revealing what the world can be like when his love reigns in human hearts.

As followers of Jesus, we're not left to do good works alone. Instead, we're empowered by God's love. The presence of God's Spirit in us flows through us like a river, spilling over into kindness, compassion, and generosity toward others. Loving others is the fruit of the Spirit of God in our lives (Galatians 5:22-23). Our good deeds are a sign, a pointer, to the heart of God. Acts of mercy are not just about being kind, but about genuinely caring for others' wellbeing. We want to follow God's command to walk in humility as we pursue justice. Loving others is obedience to the Way of Jesus (Mark 12:31).

In today's world, acts of kindness are often seen as isolated gestures. But as Christians, we believe our good works signify something more significant—the coming kingdom of God. Through our actions, we bear witness to the kingdom of God in our lives. We preview the world where love, justice, and mercy reign. We follow the pattern of prayer given to us by Jesus: "Your kingdom come, your will be done, on earth as it is in heaven" (Matthew 6:10).

REFLECTION QUESTIONS

1. **How do you understand the purpose of good works in your Christian faith?** Reflect on the role of good works in your faith. Consider how your understanding aligns with the idea that good works are an overflow of God's love working in and through you rather than a means to earn salvation.

2. **Can you think of any misconceptions about why Christians do good works that you've encountered or held in the past?** How have these misconceptions been addressed or corrected in your faith journey?

3. **Reflect on how pursuing justice and showing mercy can serve as a sign of the kingdom of God. How does this change your perspective on good deeds?** Consider how viewing good works as a demonstration of God's kingdom influences your actions and motivations. How does this perspective affect your daily approach to loving and serving your neighbors?

SCRIPTURE REFERENCES

- Proverbs 19:17
- Micah 6:8
- Matthew 5:16
  Matthew 22:37-39
- John 13:34-35
- Romans 12:9-13
- 1 Corinthians 13:3
- Galatians 5:13-14, 22-23
- Ephesians 2:10
- Colossians 3:23
- Hebrews 13:16
- James 2:14-17
- 1 Peter 4:8-10
- 1 John 3:18

QUESTION 46

What Is Worship?

ANSWER

Worship is the devotion we offer up to whatever we love most. Everyone worships. Christian worship is a lifelong outpouring of love to God, in humble adoration. Entranced by his beauty, we exalt him through praise and obedience.

"IN OUR HYPER-SECULAR WORLD, worship is still inevitable," writes novelist John Green. "But it is vital to remember that our gods don't choose us, we choose them."[1]

Green is right. Everyone worships. Worship isn't limited to activities considered religious. Worship is part of our human experience. Whether consciously or not, we all offer our adoration and devotion to something. The apostle Paul tells us how people exchange the truth about God for a lie, worshipping and serving created things rather than the Creator (Romans 1:25). Recognizing this universal aspect of worship underscores its significance in our lives. We either worship God or we worship idols. An idol is anything that absorbs your heart and imagination more than God. Idols aren't just stone statues (the instinctive image for a modern person). Idols are the thoughts, desires, longings, and expectations we worship in place of the true God.

The Bible tells the story of God's people struggling between idolatry and the worship of God. If we don't worship God, we will worship created things. In the garden of Eden, Adam and Eve were tempted to "be like God" and to make an idol out of self (Genesis 3:5). The Ten Commandments are all, in some form or another, prohibitions against idolatry. The kings in the Old Testament were tasked with purifying the land of idols, but some fell prey to idolatry. The prophets of the Old Testament raged against idolatry as well. Isaiah, Jeremiah, and Ezekiel leveled serious accusations of idolatry against God's people.

There is a fundamental difference between Christian worship, which acknowledges God's supreme worth, and idolatry, which wrongly places that worth on created things. Christian worship is an act of devotion that directs our weight, metaphorically and spiritually, toward God. The weightiness of who God is draws our love, much like an anchor that pulls us toward the bottom of a sea of worship. Christian worship is the heartfelt response to God's supreme worthiness, holiness, and unchanging nature. As William Temple once said, it involves the submission of our entire being to God—our conscience enlivened by his holiness, our mind nourished by his truth, our imagination purified by his beauty, our heart opened to his love, and our will surrendered to his purpose.[2] This outpouring of adoration is the antidote to our inherent self-centeredness and the source of all genuine goodness.

Christian worship is about grounding the weight and worth of our lives in God. This act of devotion is a continuous journey and a lifelong commitment. Our worship involves humble adoration, recognizing God's supremacy and our dependence on him. Our worship is marked by awe and wonder at God's beauty. Psalm 29:2 encourages us to "ascribe to the Lord the glory due to his name; worship the Lord in the splendor of holiness." We become what we worship. As we worship God, we become more like him, and his beauty marks our lives.

REFLECTION QUESTIONS

1. **What are some common signs of worship (acts of devotion) that take place in our world today, outside the church? What are some everyday objects of worship in our culture today?** Reflect on the various things that people, including yourself, may give ultimate worth and devotion to. Consider how these objects of worship compare to God.

2. **What are some ways you can deepen your understanding of Christian worship as a lifelong outpouring of love to God?** Think about how you can grow in your daily worship of God, making it a

continuous and holistic part of your life. What practices or changes can you implement to keep God at the center of your adoration and devotion?

3. **What role does humility play in your worship of God? Are there areas in your life where you struggle with pride that may restrict your worship of God?** Reflect on the importance of humility and identify areas where pride may hinder your complete devotion to God. Consider practical steps to cultivate humility and approach God with honesty.

SCRIPTURE REFERENCES

- 1 Chronicles 16:29
- Psalm 29:2
  Psalm 95:6-7
  Psalm 96:9
  Psalm 100:2-3
- Isaiah 6:1-3
- Matthew 22:37-38
- John 4:23-34
- Romans 12:1-2
- 1 Corinthians 6:19-20
- Philippians 2:9-11
- Hebrews 12:28-29
- Revelation 4:11

PART 7

Future Hope

Future hope addresses the Christian perspective on life beyond the present world, encompassing beliefs about life after death, final judgment, and the ultimate destiny of believers. This section explores the profound hope that sustains Christians as we navigate the present and anticipate the future.

When we die, we do not cease to exist; instead, our spirits go to be with Christ while our bodies rest until the resurrection. The Christian hope includes the promise of bodily resurrection, where believers will be raised to eternal life in the presence of God, free from sin and death. Those who oppose God will experience eternal judgment in hell—a state of existence apart from God's presence, where there is no life or light. This doctrine underscores the gravity of rejecting God's grace and highlights the urgency of repentance and faith in Christ.

Living in light of the end means ordering our lives according to the certainty of Christ's return and the coming of God's kingdom. Christians are called to live with a heavenly perspective, prioritizing eternal values over temporal concerns. This mindset encourages faithful discipleship, mission, and the pursuit of holiness.

To lean into our future hope is to look beyond the immediate and visible, grounding our faith in God's promises concerning the unseen world, life after death, and the ultimate fulfillment of his redemptive plan. This hope shapes how Christians live, endure suffering, and engage with the world as we await the glorious return of our Savior.

QUESTION 47

What Happens When We Die?

ANSWER

When we die, we do not cease to exist, neither do we become stars or angels. Our spirits soar to Christ our hope in life and death, and our bodies rest until the resurrection.

THERE'S A COMMON MISCONCEPTION about Christianity that says our future hope consists of disembodied souls occupying an ethereal heaven when we die. A lot of ideas commonly associated with Christianity and the afterlife are wrongheaded. The goal of the afterlife, for the Christian, is not to escape this earth and get to heaven. The goal is actually for heaven to come to earth and for the two to be reunited at last. The idea of leaving this world and enjoying forever a nonbodily existence does not have a place in Christianity. It more closely resembles ancient Gnostic teachings the church rightly rejected!

The New Testament does not describe heaven—where our spirits go when we die—as our ultimate hope or the long-term future. The heavenly afterlife is more like a hotel, a place for our souls to rejoice in God while our bodies rest, before the round-trip journey back to a renewed earth in resurrected splendor. Rightly understood, salvation is not a rescue *from* creation, it's the rescue *of* creation.

The Christian vision of death counters popular understandings in at least two ways. First, the Christian vision counters the widespread belief that death is the end, and that nonexistence is all that follows. Secular narratives are closed off to the possibility of God or an unseen realm and simply conclude that death means we cease to exist. The Christian perspective is that death is not annihilation. There is life after death. "I am the resurrection and the life," Jesus said. "The one who believes in me, even if he dies, will live. Everyone who lives and believes in me will never die" (John 11:25-26).

Second, Christianity counters the idea that we turn into stars or angels after death. We will not be transformed into celestial entities when we die or morph into ethereal beings. The ultimate future for the Christian is the resurrection of the body and the restoration of this world. All who trust in Jesus Christ will receive a new body when he returns.

The God who made the world is sovereign over death and beyond; death can't challenge what God will bring. When Christians die, our spirits ascend to be with Jesus. Christ is our source of hope both in life and death. After death, we will experience a two-stage postmortem reality. First, our souls will rest with Jesus Christ and experience refreshment. Second, we will be bodily resurrected, soul and body will be united, and we will live with God on a new earth.

According to the Bible, God's work of redemption was concerned with healing and restoring the world, "For God so loved the world" (John 3:16). Jesus said, "My kingdom is not of this world" (18:36), meaning that his kingdom doesn't come *from* this world, but his kingdom is very much *for* this world. Salvation is about God rescuing his people and his world from the ravages of sin and death. Paul tells us the last enemy—death—will be swallowed up in victory (1 Corinthians 15:20-22).

REFLECTION QUESTIONS

1. **How does the concept of a bodily resurrection challenge common misconceptions—both inside and outside of the church—about the afterlife?** Discuss how this understanding contrasts with widespread beliefs about becoming angels or ceasing to exist and what this implies about the nature of eternal life.

2. **Why is it significant for Christians to acknowledge death does not lead to nonexistence?** Explore this belief 's theological and

existential implications and how it impacts how Christians view death.

3. **In what ways does the Christian vision of death provide hope and comfort in the face of mortality and grief?** Reflect on how the promise of being with Christ immediately after death and the future resurrection offers a unique perspective on dealing with the loss of loved ones and the reality of our mortality.

SCRIPTURE REFERENCES

- Job 19:25-27
- Ecclesiastes 12:7
- Daniel 12:2
- John 11:25-26
- Romans 8:11
- 1 Corinthians 15:20-23, 42-44, 51-53
- 2 Corinthians 5:8
- Philippians 1:21-23 Philippians 3:20-21
- 1 Thessalonians 4:16-17
- 1 Peter 1:3-4
- Revelation 14:13

QUESTION 48

What Happens to Those Who Oppose God?

ANSWER

God will one day purge the world of evil and establish righteousness on earth. Those who oppose God will experience eternal judgment—an everlasting fate apart from him, where his life and light are no more.

JOHN LENNON'S 1971 SONG "IMAGINE" invites us to envision a world without heaven and hell, where living for today is all that matters. This anthem captures the spirit of the post-1960s era of questioning traditional beliefs and values. "Imagine" wants a world of peace and harmony, but it's hard to see how such a world could exist apart from some notion of fairness and justice. Lennon's vision eliminates heaven and hell but leaves us without answers for life's brokenness. Some of the very people who express frustration with God for not making everything right in this world right away also despise any notion of God executing judgment on evil.

Christianity offers a refreshing and startling word to a world that imagines life without eternal consequences. To the one who longs for justice and yet doesn't think God should judge, Christianity says: *You can't have it both ways.*

The Bible acknowledges the present world's injustices but points to a future where all wrongs will be righted, justice will prevail, and God will hold all accountable. This is why in the Old Testament, when the psalmist talks about the judgment of God, he rejoices (Psalm 96). Not because he is filled with contempt for others or thinks he deserves eternal life, but because he wants to see justice enacted, the oppressed delivered, and the world restored. Likewise, in the New Testament, the truth of King Jesus returning to this world to judge the living and the dead brings great comfort to all who are persecuted (2 Timothy 4:1).

Deep down, we want God to make the world right. We want God to fix everything. We want a world of perfect justice. But our desire for perfection runs into a point of contradiction. If God eradicates evil and establishes a perfect world, where does that leave us? We not only suffer under the fallenness of this world; we've done our share of contributing to it. Even though we long for God to right everything in the world, we must acknowledge we're part of what is wrong with the world.

God's ultimate plan is to restore his good creation now marred by sin. To do so, God must and will eradicate evil from the world and establish perfect righteousness. This means, all who oppose God and remain on the side of evil will face eternal judgment, a truth that highlights the gravity of rebellion against God.

Eternal judgment is the consequence of opposing God. Turning our backs on God is what separates us from God's life and light. Many people today struggle with the idea of hell and the images Jesus used to describe this everlasting fate. But we should receive the warnings of Scripture as an expression of God's love, a warning to us that the act of severing ourselves from God, the source of life, results in eternal death. Uprooting ourselves from the soil leaves only the scorching heat to wither us eternally. Only in Christ, the True Vine, is life to be found.

Sin leads to severing, and this separation underscores the severity of the choice to rebel against the Creator and Judge. In the final judgment, righteousness and goodness will prevail. That's why now is the time to recognize the gravity of sin, turn from sin to Jesus in faith, and be safe with him on that day when he returns to execute justice.

REFLECTION QUESTIONS

1. **Why do you think many people today struggle with accepting the idea of final judgment and hell?** Explore the cultural and philosophical reasons behind the resistance to these concepts and how they contrast with the biblical view of justice and eternal judgment.

2. **How does the loss of focus on eternal judgment or God's holiness diminish our understanding of God's grace and love?** Discuss how neglecting the truth about what our sins deserve can minimize the depth and significance of God's grace and the sacrificial love demonstrated through Jesus Christ.

3. **How does the holiness on display in the final judgment shape our present understanding of mercy?** Reflect on how an awareness of our sinfulness and need for redemption shapes our perception of God's judgment and the profound mercy offered through Christ's sacrifice.

SCRIPTURE REFERENCES

- Isaiah 65:17
- Daniel 12:2
- Matthew 13:49-50
  Matthew 25:41-46
- John 3:16
  John 3:36
- Romans 2:5-7
  Romans 6:23
- 2 Corinthians 5:10
- Hebrews 10:26-27
- 2 Peter 3:13
- Revelation 20:11-15
  Revelation 21:4
  Revelation 22:20

QUESTION 49

What Is the Ultimate Hope for the Christian?

ANSWER

Our hope is Jesus Christ. We believe he will come again to reign over and restore the world, delighting to dwell with us and grant life everlasting, forever filling us with wonder, love, and praise.

"A MAN WHO BELIEVES IS a man who hopes," claimed Nicolas Sarkozy, former president of France. "Secular morality always risks exhausting itself because it is not backed up by a hope that fulfills man's aspirations for the infinite."[1]

Our world wants to hope but doesn't know how. We place our faith in ourselves and believe in the promises we make about human achievement. We modify and apply the best practices of religion and philosophy while resisting the call to open ourselves up to the real possibility of faith in God. We settle for false hopes that give us the illusion of reality. Like drinking in the sea to satisfy our thirst, we only leave ourselves more parched.

The Bible holds out a uniquely Christian vision of hope. Professor Vinoth Ramachandra says, "No faith holds out a promise of eternal salvation for the world the way the cross and resurrection of Jesus do."[2] The author of Hebrews says faith is the assurance of what we hope for and the certainty of things we cannot see (Hebrews 11:1-2). It's not a tentative desire; it's anchored in God's unwavering promises. Philosopher and theologian John Frame puts it beautifully, "Hope is not something radically different from faith, but it is a kind of faith: faith directed toward the future fulfillment of the purposes of God."[3] Faith and hope come together; faith focuses on God's authority through his Word, and hope looks to his sovereignty and knows God will bring his Word to pass.

We were created to live for God and to hope in God. If we fail to live for God, we will be driven by the other things we live for. One of the terrible consequences of sin is that we fail to make God our greatest hope. We try to maintain control of our lives by pursuing money, success, status, sex, comfort, or something else. The result is always a loss of power, a form of slavery. We do not steal, commit adultery, or hurt people unless we first make something more fundamental to our hope and joy than our identity in God.

The ultimate hope for the Christian is embodied in Jesus Christ. He is not just the fulfillment of God's promises; he is our hope. Christians look back at the fulfilled promises of God and look ahead to the eventual return of Jesus Christ. We expect his glorious return, where he will reign and restore the world to its original perfection. In his presence, we will find eternal life and limitless joy. The new heavens and earth will one day be our eternal home. We will be free from suffering and sorrow. All that will remain is the presence of God filling us evermore with wonder, love, and unending praise.

REFLECTION QUESTIONS

1. **How does hope in Christianity differ from mere optimism or wishful thinking?** Consider the depth and foundation of Christian hope, distinguishing it from general positive thinking by highlighting its basis in God's promises and sovereignty.

2. **How does Jesus's resurrection shape our understanding of hope?** What does it look like to anchor Christian hope in the historical and transformative event of Jesus's resurrection, and the assurance of our future resurrection and eternal life with him?

3. **In what ways does the Christian understanding of hope provide strength and endurance during life's trials and uncertainties?** Consider the practical impact of Christian hope, and how the assurance of God's promises and the anticipation of Christ's return equip believers to face challenges with resilience and faith.

SCRIPTURE REFERENCES

- Psalm 33:20
  Psalm 42:11
  Psalm 71:14
  Psalm 147:11
- Isaiah 40:31
- Jeremiah 29:11
- John 14:2-3
- Romans 5:5
  Romans 8:24-25
  Romans 15:13
- 1 Corinthians 15:19
- 2 Corinthians 5:1
- Colossians 1:27
- 1 Thessalonians 4:16-17
- 1 Timothy 4:10
- Titus 2:13
- Hebrews 6:19
  Hebrews 11:1
- 1 Peter 1:3
- Revelation 21:1-4
  Revelation 22:3-5

QUESTION 50

What Does It Mean to Live in Light of the End?

ANSWER

We walk by faith, not in secular progress and technological advance, but in the promise of God to reclaim this world and make everything right. With hope, we await the return of the King we love.

IN A WORLD OFTEN CONSUMED by the allure of secular progress and the relentless march of technological advance, the prevailing question becomes, "What's next?" Many find themselves caught in the narrative of unending human achievement, constantly seeking the next big thing.

The world often adopts different "eschatologies"—stories of human progress toward the future—that people cling to for meaning and hope. There's the Enlightenment eschatology of science and technology, the emancipatory eschatology of the sexual revolution, and consumer society's eschatology of personal fulfillment through acquisition and personal branding.

While the world asks, "What's next?" the church asks a different question: "What time is it?" Specifically, "What does obedience and faithfulness to Jesus look like in this particular *time*?" We aim to understand our times in light of God's sovereign plan for the world. We are concerned with more than the immediate and material. We know this world belongs to God, who will make everything right. Instead of being driven by the illusion of unending progress, we live with faith and hope, countering other visions for the world by following Jesus in the here and now.

Living in light of the end means acknowledging that our lives are not just part of a linear story of human progress. We recognize the end is coming, and we order our days accordingly. This means we engage in spiritual formation and obedience that looks to the eventual end, looks around at the contemporary setting, and seeks to counter rival conceptions of time and progress.

Theologian Michael Bird puts it this way: "The resurrection of Jesus and the gift of the Spirit mean that God's new world has begun, the future has partially invaded the present, the seeds of the new creation have already begun to bud in the old garden, and God's victory on the cross is now reclaiming territory in a world enslaved by sin."[1] This reminds us that heaven isn't an escape from earthly responsibilities but is the necessary horizon or framework for the church to engage in doing good on earth. We counter other visions of the good life by living as citizens of heaven here and now, leaning into the promised future.

Why do we live with hope? Because we know our King, and because we believe his promises. We wait for him because we love him. No matter how impatient our world seems in its quest for progress, or whether people become optimistic or pessimistic in terms of technology, we can stay centered because of our hope in the promises of God.

Our world needs the hope we have. We offer that hope as people committed to the mission God has given us, seeking every opportunity to bring their outlook on the world into an encounter with the ever-powerful and all-good story told in the Scriptures.

REFLECTION QUESTIONS

1. **How can you balance living in the present while eagerly anticipating the future hope of Jesus's return?** Reflect on navigating the tension between your daily responsibilities and anticipating Jesus's return.

2. **How can you align your priorities with the eternal perspective of God's coming kingdom?** Reflect on how your current values, goals, and actions can be realigned to reflect the eternal priorities of God's

kingdom, promoting a life that is both impactful now and in light of eternity.

3. **What role does hope play in your ability to endure suffering and challenges?** Explore how the Christian hope of Jesus's return and the promise of a new heaven and new earth provide strength and resilience amid life's difficulties, fostering a deeper understanding of how hope sustains you through trials.

SCRIPTURE REFERENCES

- Isaiah 65:17
- Matthew 6:19-21
  Matthew 24:36, 42-44
- Romans 8:18
- 2 Corinthians 5:7
- Philippians 3:20-21
- Colossians 3:1-2
- 1 Thessalonians 4:16-18
- Titus 2:11-13
- Hebrews 11:13-16
- 2 Peter 3:11-13
- Revelation 21:3-5

APPENDIX

The Ten Commandments

I am the Lord your God, who brought you out of the land of Egypt, out of the place of slavery.

Do not have other gods besides me.

Do not make an idol for yourself in the shape of anything in the heavens above or on the earth below or in the waters under the earth. Do not bow in worship to them, and do not serve them, because I, the Lord your God, am a jealous God, bringing the consequences of the fathers' iniquity on the children to the third and fourth generations of those who hate me, but showing faithful love to a thousand generations of those who love me and keep my commands.

Do not misuse the name of the Lord your God, because the Lord will not leave anyone unpunished who misuses his name.

Be careful to remember the Sabbath day, to keep it holy as the Lord your God has commanded you. You are to labor six days and do all your work, but the seventh day is a Sabbath to the Lord your God. Do not do any work—you, your son or daughter, your male or female slave, your ox or donkey, any of your livestock, or the resident alien who lives within your city gates, so that your male and female slaves may rest as you do. Remember that you were a slave in the land of Egypt, and the Lord your God brought you out of there with a strong hand and an outstretched arm. That is why the Lord your God has commanded you to keep the Sabbath day.

Honor your father and your mother, as the Lord your God has commanded you, so that you may live long and so that you may prosper in the land the Lord your God is giving you.

Do not murder.

Do not commit adultery.

Do not steal.

Do not give dishonest testimony against your neighbor.

Do not covet your neighbor's wife or desire your neighbor's house, his field, his male or female slave, his ox or donkey, or anything that belongs to your neighbor.

(Exodus 20:2-17)

The Lord's Prayer

Our Father in heaven,
  hallowed be your name,
your kingdom come,
your will be done
  on earth as it is in heaven.
Give us this day our daily bread.
And forgive us our debts
  as we also have forgiven our debtors.
And lead us not into temptation,
  but deliver us from the evil one.
For yours is the kingdom and
the power and the glory forever. Amen.

(Matthew 6:9-13 NIV)

The Apostles' Creed

I believe in God, the Father almighty,
creator of heaven and earth;
I believe in Jesus Christ, his only Son, our Lord.
He was conceived by the power of the Holy Spirit
and born of the Virgin Mary.
He suffered under Pontius Pilate,
was crucified, died, and was buried.
He descended to the dead.
On the third day he rose again.
He ascended into heaven,
and is seated at the right hand of the Father.
He will come again to judge the living and the dead.
I believe in the Holy Spirit,
the holy catholic Church,
the communion of saints,
the forgiveness of sins
the resurrection of the body,
and the life everlasting. Amen.

Definitions of the Gospel

At its briefest, the gospel is a discourse about Christ, that he is the Son of God and became man for us, that he died and was raised, and that he has been established as Lord over all things... There you have it. The gospel is a story about Christ, God's and David's son, who died and was raised, and is established as Lord. This is the gospel in a nutshell.[1]

—Martin Luther

Evangelion (that we call the gospel) is a Greek word and signifieth good, merry, glad and joyful tidings, that maketh a man's heart glad and maketh him sing, dance, and leap for joy... [This gospel is] all of Christ the right David, how that he hath fought with sin, with death, and the devil, and overcome them: whereby all men that were in bondage to sin, wounded with death, overcome of the devil are without their own merits or deservings loosed, justified, restored to life and saved, brought to liberty and reconciled unto the favor of God and set at one with him again: which tidings as many as believe laud, praise and thank God, are glad, sing and dance for joy.[2]

—William Tyndale

I formulate the Gospel this way: it is information issuing in invitation; it is proclamation issuing in persuasion. It is an admonitory message embracing five themes. First, God: the God whom Paul proclaimed to the Athenians in Acts 17, the God of Christian theism. Second, humankind: made in God's image but now totally unable to respond to God or do anything right by reason of sin in their moral and spiritual system. Third, the person and work of Christ: God incarnate, who by dying wrought atonement and who now lives to impart the blessing

> that flows form his work of atonement. Fourth, repentance, that is, turning from sin to God, from self-will to Jesus Christ. And fifthly, new community: a new family, a new pattern of human togetherness which results from the unity of the Lord's people in the Lord, henceforth to function under the one Father as a family and a fellowship.[3]
>
> —J.I. Packer

> That the gospel is the good news that the triune God has poured out his grace in the life, death, resurrection, and ascension of the Lord Jesus Christ, so that through his work we might have peace with God (Rom. 5:1). Jesus lived in perfect obedience yet suffered everything sinners deserved so that sinners would not have to pursue a righteousness of their own, relying on their own works, but rather through trust in him as the fulfillment of God's promises could be justified by faith alone (*sola fide*) in order to become fellow heirs with him. Christ died in the place of sinners, absorbing the wages of sin (Rom. 6:23), so that those who entrust themselves to him also die with him to the power, penalty, and (eventually) practice of sin. Christ was raised the firstborn of a renewed and restored creation, so that those whom the Spirit unites to him in faith are raised up and created a new humanity in him (Eph. 2:15). Renewed in God's image, they are thereby enabled to live out his life in them. One with Christ and made alive in him who is the only ground of salvation, sinners are reconciled with God—justified, adopted, sanctified, and eventually glorified children of the promise.[4]
>
> —The Reforming Catholic Confession, 2017

The Gospel Proper (The Announcement)

The gospel is the royal announcement that Jesus Christ, the Son of God, lived a perfect life in our place, died a substitutionary death on the cross for our sins, rose triumphantly from the grave to launch God's new creation, and is now exalted as King of the world. This announcement calls for a response: repentance (mourning over and turning from our sin, trading our agendas for the kingdom agenda of Jesus Christ) and faith (trusting in Christ alone for salvation).

The Gospel's Context (The Story of Scripture)

The Bible tells us about God's creation of a good world which was subjected to futility because of human sin. God gave the Law to reveal his holiness and our need for a perfect sacrifice, which is provided by the death of Jesus Christ. This same Jesus will one day return to this earth to judge the living and the dead and thus renew all things. The gospel story is the scriptural narrative that takes us from creation to new creation, climaxing with the death and resurrection of Jesus at the center.

The Gospel's Purpose (The Community)

The gospel births the church. We are shaped by the gospel into the kind of people who herald the grace of God and spread the news of Jesus Christ. God has commissioned the church to be the community that embodies the message of the gospel. Through our corporate life together, we "obey the gospel" by living according to the truth of the message that Jesus Christ is Savior and Lord of the world.

All Together Now

> Put these three things together and we have a gospel-focused summary of the entire Bible.
>
> In the beginning, the all-powerful, personal God created the universe. This God created human beings in His image to live joyfully in His presence, in humble submission to His gracious authority. But all of us have rebelled against God and, in consequence, must suffer the punishment of our rebellion: physical death and the wrath of God.
>
> Thankfully, God initiated a rescue plan, which began with His choosing the nation of Israel to display His glory in a fallen world. The Bible describes how God acted mightily on Israel's behalf, rescuing His people from slavery and then giving them His holy law. But God's people—like all of us—failed to rightly reflect the glory of God.
>
> Then, in the fullness of time, in the Person of Jesus Christ, God Himself came to renew the world and restore His people. Jesus perfectly obeyed the law given to Israel. Though innocent, He suffered the consequences of human rebellion by His death on a cross. But three days later, God raised Him from the dead.

Now the church of Jesus Christ has been commissioned by God to take the news of Christ's work to the world. Empowered by God's Spirit, the church calls all people everywhere to repent of sin and to trust in Christ alone for our forgiveness. Repentance and faith restores our relationship with God and results in a life of ongoing transformation.

The Bible promises that Jesus Christ will return to this earth as the conquering King. Only those who live in repentant faith in Christ will escape God's judgment and live joyfully in God's presence for all eternity. God's message is the same to all of us: repent and believe, before it is too late. Confess with your mouth that Jesus is Lord and believe in your heart that God raised Him from the dead, and you will be saved.[5]

–Trevin Wax

Notes

Introduction

1. Lesslie Newbigin, *Unfinished Agenda: An Updated Autobiography* (Wipf and Stock, 2009), 228.
2. Lesslie Newbigin, *Foolishness to the Greeks: The Gospel and Western Culture* (Wm. B. Eerdmans, 1988), 41.
3. Trevin Wax, *Rethink Your Self: The Power of Looking Up Before Looking In* (B&H Books, 2020).
4. Lesslie Newbigin, *The Open Secret: An Introduction to the Theology of Mission* (Wm. B. Eerdmans, 1995), 27.
5. Timothy Keller, *How to Reach the West Again: Six Essential Elements of a Missionary Encounter* (Redeemer City to City, 2020), 38.
6. Tim Keller, "The Decline and Renewal of the American Church: Part 4—The Strategy for Renewal," Gospel in Life, https://quarterly.gospelinlife.com/american-church-the-strategy-for-renewal/.

Question 1: What Is the Center and Point of Everything?

1. William Ernest Henly, "Invictus," written in 1875. This poem is in the public domain.
2. Charles Taylor, *A Secular Age* (Belknap, 2018), 38.

Question 2: How Do We See God and Come to Know Him?

1. *Stanford Encyclopedia of Philosophy*, s.v. "Protagoras," first published September 8, 2020, https://plato.stanford.edu/entries/protagoras/.
2. John Calvin also used this metaphor when he said, "Just as old or bleary-eyed men and those with weak vision, if you thrust before them a most beautiful volume, even if they recognize it to be some sort of writing, yet can scarcely construe two words, but with the aid of spectacles will begin to read distinctly; so Scripture, gathering up the otherwise confused knowledge of God in our minds, having dispersed our dullness, clearly shows us the true God." John Calvin, *Institutes of the Christian Religion*, vol. 1, ed. John T. McNeill, trans. Ford Lewis Battles (Westminster, 1960), 69-70.

Question 4: Who Is God the Father?

1. Michael Reeves, *Delighting in The Trinity: An Introduction to the Christian Faith* (IVP Academic, 2012), 57.

Question 6: Who Is God the Spirit?

1. The Westminster Standard, Larger Catechism: Text and Scripture Proofs, https://thewestminsterstandard.org/westminster-larger-catechism/.

Question 7: Why Did God Create the World?

1. IMDb, "*Cosmos* Quotes," https://www.imdb.com/title/tt0081846/quotes/?ref_=tt_dyk_qu.
2. Carl Sagan, 1980s miniseries *Cosmos*.
3. The common refrain "god of the gaps" first appears in *Science and Christian Belief* by Charles Alfred Coulson (Oxford University Press, 1955), 20.

Question 9: Why Did God Create Us?

1. Michael Allan Gillespie, *The Theological Origins of Modernity* (University of Chicago Press, 2009), 276.

Question 11: What Is Sexuality?

1. Ben White, "Ex-GI Becomes Blonde Beauty: Operations Transform Bronx Youth," *New York Daily News*, December 1, 1952.

Question 21: What Is Suffering?

1. Max Scheler, *The Meaning of Suffering* (Martinus Nijhoff, 1974), 61.

Question 23: What Do We Learn from Israel's Sacrificial System?

1. Christian D. Larson, *Your Forces and How to Use Them* (Zinc Read, 2023), 21.
2. Oprah Winfrey, "Oprah Winfrey's 2008 Stanford Commencement Address," June 15, 2008, YouTube video, 29:54, https://www.youtube.com/watch?v=Bpd3raj8xww.

Question 27: What Happened on the Cross?

1. Plato, *Five Dialogues*, trans. Benjamin Jowett (Philosophy Classics, 2018), 144. This work was first published as *The Dialogues of Plato*, 5 vols. in 1892.

Question 28: What Happened on Easter?

1. Justin Taylor, "85 Years Ago Today: J.R.R. Tolkien Convinces C. S. Lewis That Christ Is the True Myth," The Gospel Coalition, September 20, 2016, https://www.thegospelcoalition.org/blogs/evangelical-history/85-years-ago-today-j-r-r-tolkien-convinces-c-s-lewis-that-christ-is-the-true-myth/.

Question 31: What Is Repentance?

1. *Martin Luther's Basic Theological Writings*, 3rd ed., "The Ninety-Five Theses (1517)," ed. Timothy F. Lull and William R. Russell (Fortress, 2012), 8.

Question 33: What Is Union with Christ?

1. John Calvin, *Commentary on Ephesians*, chap. V.32, cited in Marcus Peter Johnson, *One with Christ: An Evangelical Theology of Salvation* (Crossway, 2013), 49.

Question 36: What Is Glorification?

1. Samuel Fishwick, "Transhumanism: The Final Frontier?", *The Standard*, September 29, 2022, https://www.standard.co.uk/lifestyle/transhumanism-science-humans-robots-final-frontier-b1028526.html.

Question 37: What Is the Kingdom of God?

1. Michael Foucault covers this in his book, *Religion and Culture*, selected and edited by Jeremy R. Carrette (Routledge, 1999).

Question 40: What Is the Lord's Supper?

1. William Leach, *Land of Desire: Merchants, Power, and the Rise of a New American Culture* (Pantheon, 1993), 3.

Question 44: Why Do We Tell People about Jesus?

1. Yaagneshwaran Ganesh, host, *The Yaag Project Podcast*, podcast, season 1, episode 66, "Guy Kawasaki: What being a product evangelist means," March 1, 2021, https://the-yaag-project.simplecast.com/episodes/guy-kawasaki-what-being-a-product-evangelist-means-utDD_Uy_.

Question 46: What Is Worship?

1. John Green, *The Anthropocene Reviewed: Essays on a Human-Centered Planet* (Dutton, 2021), 195.
2. William Temple, quoted in Warren W. Wiersbe, *The Integrity Crisis* (Thomas Nelson, 1991), 119.

Question 49: What Is the Ultimate Hope for the Christian?

1. Speech delivered at Palace of St. John Lateran, 2005. See New Humanist, "Hope Against Hope," https://newhumanist.org.uk/articles/2828/hope-against-hope.
2. Vinoth Ramachandra, *The Scandal of Jesus* (InterVarsity, 2001), 24.
3. John Frame, *Systematic Theology: An Introduction to Christian Belief* (P&R, 2013), 332.

Question 50: What Does It Mean to Live in Light of the End?

1. Michael Bird, *Evangelical Theology: A Biblical and Systematic Introduction* (Zondervan, 2013), 827.

Appendix: Definitions of the Gospel

1. *Martin Luther's Basic Theological Writings*, 3rd ed., "Preface to the New Testament (1522, Revised 1546)," ed. Timothy F. Lull and William R. Russell (Fortress, 2012), 94.
2. William Tyndale, "A Pathway into the Holy Scriptures," in Doctrinal Treatises and Introductions to Different Portions of the Holy Scriptures (Cambridge University Press, 1848), 8.
3. J.I. Packer, *Serving the People of God: Collected Shorter Writings of J.I. Packer*, Vol. 2. (Paternoster, 1998), 44.
4. The Reforming Catholic Confession was published in 2017 to mark the 500th anniversary of Martin Luther's posting of his 95 Theses to the door of the Castle Church in Wittenberg. To read the full confession, see "A Reforming Catholic Confession," https://reformingcatholicconfession.com.
5. The Gospel Project, see also Trevin Wax, *Gospel Centered Teaching: Showing Christ in All the Scriptures* (Broadman & Holman), 39-41, 49-50.

Acknowledgments

We are grateful for all the feedback and assistance we've received as we've worked on this project. A special thank you to the C.S. Lewis Foundation which owns The Kilns, where on a sunny November day in 2022, the initial outline of this project was born. Thanks also to the many scholars and pastors who gave us substantive feedback along the way, including Kevin Vanhoozer, Bob Thune, Andrew Wilson, Brandon Smith, Derek Rishmawy, Justin Schell, Matt Smethurst, Ivan Mesa, Jeremy Treat, Gavin Ortlund, Josh Chatraw, Keith Plummer, Noah Oldham, J.D. Greear, Ronjour Locke, and Jon Tyson. Thank you to Michael Card for his help in styling. A special thank you to the team at Harvest House Publishers, especially Audrey Greeson for her vision for this project.